Wavelength

A handbook of communication strategies for working with young people

Josie Melia

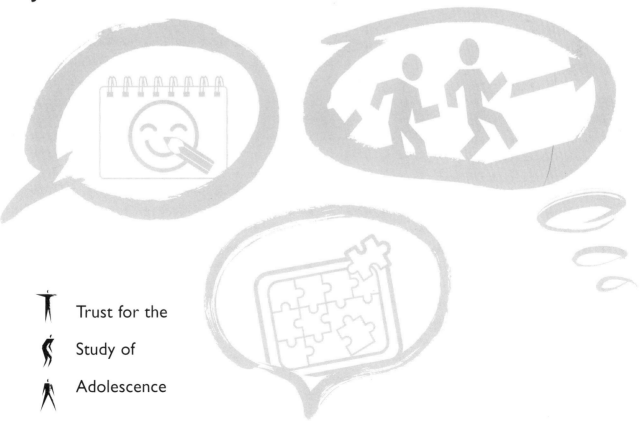

Trust for the

Study of

Adolescence

Contents

Foreword

It gives me great pleasure to be able to write a foreword to this excellent and timely publication. Issues to do with communication between adults and young people have long been a focus of the work of TSA, and thus it is particularly appropriate that Josie Melia, together with Kevin Lowe, have produced this resource for practitioners.

This publication is one of a long line of resources to do with communication issues that have been produced by TSA, including videos for parents, as well as videos and training packs for professionals. Some years ago we produced *Getting Through*, our first pack on communication skills for workers with young people, and this has been followed by other resources, including our best-selling training pack developed by Josie Melia and Marilyn McGowan, entitled *Working with Young People*.

Wavelength is thus the outcome of a long tradition of interest in, and concern with, finding ways to assist adults in being able to communicate effectively with young people. This new resource contains a combination of two essential elements — an introduction to knowledge and understanding of the principles of communication with young people, followed by a treasure store of tips, ideas and techniques for actually working with young people in a manner that will facilitate good communication. I have no doubt at all that it will prove as successful as previous publications sold by TSA, and I commend it to all who work with young people, no matter what the setting. We are grateful to the Department of Health for funding enabling us to develop these materials, and personally I wish to thank Josie and Kevin for the dedication and hard work that has gone into the development of this exciting new publication.

John Coleman
Director, TSA

Acknowledgements

This handbook reflects TSA s ongoing work on young people and communication. It brings together strategies and activities used by professionals from many different contexts. I would like to thank all those who have shared their ideas with me, either in practice or on training events and conferences run by TSA.

I would particularly like to thank at TSA, Kevin Lowe for his input, editing and encouragement, John Coleman and Jayne Hellett for commenting on draft material and Catrin Prosser for collating the information about resources and suppliers. Special thanks also to Helen Beauvais of Creative Media Colour for her creativity and flexibility in designing and preparing this for publication, Marilyn McGowan, Lyn Coorg and many others for their inspirational approaches to work with young people.

Josie Melia

Introduction

What is this book about?

This book is about ways of engaging with young people for different purposes and in different settings, with the overall aim of supporting and empowering the young people involved.

Communication is at the heart of *Wavelength*, whether it be through the use of the written word or visuals, by moving sorting and handling or through drama and other activities.

Workers from different professional settings each have their own approaches and techniques but may feel stuck from time to time, when the usual approaches aren t reaching particular individuals, or when a group seems bored with these methods. This handbook is intended to be a resource for workers when they reach those stuck moments in their work. It includes techniques and approaches from a variety of professional settings, such as youth work, youth arts, social work and counselling. It aims to share examples of different ways of working and encourage workers to use their creativity to apply new styles to their own work.

What is it not?

This is not a handbook of photocopiable activity sheets. It describes many techniques and demonstrates how ideas can be adapted so that different techniques achieve the same aims. For example, it may show a worker how an activity she usually presents via paired discussion can also be done by getting young people moving around working out a puzzle together.

The handbook is also not a complete guide to communicating with young people. It builds on the work of TSA s training and resource packs *Working with Young People: developing professional practice in interpersonal, communication and counselling skills* and *Listening in Colour* (created by Youth Access) which focus in detail on the qualities, values, ethics and skills involved in working with young people. *Wavelength* is a collection of approaches and techniques to be used by professionals who know about working with young people and want to vary the repertoire of activities they use to engage with them on topics relevant to their work.

Who is it for?

This handbook is useful for a range of workers. They may be social workers, leaving care workers, foster carers, befrienders, supported housing staff, youth offending team workers, Connexions workers, nurses who work with young people, other health workers, counsellors, mentors, teachers and pastoral staff in schools, youth arts practitioners, members of youth offending teams and others whose work brings them into contact with young people as individuals or groups.

Wavelength supports National Occupational Standards in several different occupational sectors. Some examples follow. The list is not comprehensive, simply an indication of the scope of relevant units:

Elements within the following units of the **National Occupational Standards for Youth Work (Paulo):**

A1. Establish relationships and maintain dialogue with young people

A2. Enable young people to access information and make decisions

B1. Enable young people to explore and develop their values and self-respect

B3. Enable young people to work effectively in groups

C1. Work with young people to design and develop sessions

C3. Review progress and evaluate opportunities with young people

D2. Work in ways which promote equality of opportunity, participation and responsibility.

The following elements from **Health and Social Care (Children and Young People) Specific Level 4 Optional Units (TOPSS):**

HSC46a Work with the children and young people to identify how and by whom they wish to be represented

HSC46b Work with children and young people to represent their needs and wishes

HSC46c Help children and young people understand the procedures and outcomes from the representation

HSC46d Support children and young people to evaluate their experiences of the advocacy support and the systems they have encountered.

The following units from the **National Occupational Standards for Learning, Development and Support services for children and those who care for them (Connexions):**

Unit 9. Facilitate children and young people s learning and development through mentoring

Unit 11. Assist clients to gain access to other services

Unit 12. Enable children and young people to understand and address their difficulties

Unit 15. Support young people in tackling problems and taking action.

How is it organised?

Part One

After the introduction, *Wavelength* has two main parts. The first part is **Communicating with young people** which begins with an overview about communication and then looks at creating a welcoming environment together with beginning and ending working relationships. It then goes on to detail some of the skills involved in **Communicating for different purposes.** Six areas are covered:

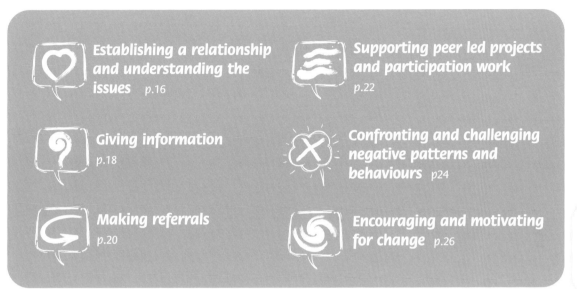

Establishing a relationship and understanding the issues p.16

Supporting peer led projects and participation work p.22

Giving information p.18

Confronting and challenging negative patterns and behaviours p24

Making referrals p.20

Encouraging and motivating for change p.26

Part Two

The second main part begins with a short introduction to **Creating and adapting your own resources** and then features examples of activities for communicating with young people. The activities are grouped into four sections, reflecting four different styles of engaging young people in learning:

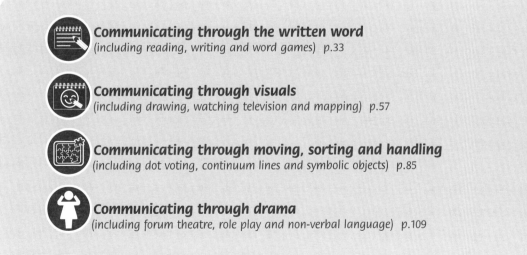

Communicating through the written word
(including reading, writing and word games) p.33

Communicating through visuals
(including drawing, watching television and mapping) p.57

Communicating through moving, sorting and handling
(including dot voting, continuum lines and symbolic objects) p.85

Communicating through drama
(including forum theatre, role play and non-verbal language) p.109

Some of the activities described fall into more than one category, but they are grouped so that you can easily find activities that are likely to work best with the favoured learning styles of the young people you are working with, and so you can mix and match activities from different sections to address a range of learning styles in a group. Communicating through sound and music is also included in some of the activities described and verbal communication is a common feature of most techniques.

A list of further resources and suppliers is at the end of the handbook.

Feel free to dip in and out of the different parts and sections of Wavelength in a way that suits you. It is not necessary to read the parts in the order they appear in the handbook. For example you may decide to go straight to the activities in part two and then return to part one to review the material on communicating for different purposes.

Part One

Communicating with young people

Communicating with young people

It is easy to take the idea of communication for granted. It is at the heart of all our interaction with other people, but it's rarely straightforward. Most people will recognise occasions when 'things just click'. They 'tune in' with another person and something starts to happen. Texts that describe positive ways of working with young people usually identify trust, respect, empathy, genuineness, warmth, flexibility and patience as central elements of positive working relationships. It would be impossible to build such relationships without effective communication.

Wavelength stems from the idea of 'tuning in' with a young person. The Chambers English Dictionary lists 'to have something in common (with another person)' as one of the meanings of the word 'communication', as well as the more common 'to succeed in conveying one's meaning to others'. The two-way nature of communication is part of the thinking behind this manual, for although it provides lots of practical tools and techniques for communicating with young people, they are all based on the notion of 'getting alongside' the young person.

Although different workers' roles affect the opportunities available to them in how they might work with a young person, the basic task of tuning in is common to all. For example, some workers will be able to get to know the young person over a long period, with much individual contact. Others may only meet the person once, or may have fleeting contact. But most of us can recall situations when we met someone once and felt respected and understood or have known someone for a long time and yet find it hard to communicate with them.

The techniques described in *Wavelength* will only be effective if they enable young people to feel that they are being valued as individuals and that their hopes and concerns are taken seriously. For this to happen it is important to recognise that effective communication is as much about attitude as it is about techniques. Adults may be anxious or even fearful of young people. It is not unusual to hear it said that 'young people's rights have gone too far', yet at the same time, many young people say that all they want is 'a little bit of respect'.

TSA's research on communication with 4,000 young people aged between 12 and 20 (*Getting Through*) identified behaviours that young people saw as signs of good communication. Examples included, 'looking as if you want to communicate', 'smiling and using eye contact' and 'focusing 100% on you'. Poor communication included the opposites such as 'not maintaining eye contact' as well as 'criticising you', 'rubbing it in' and 'insisting on having the last word'.

Users of this handbook will be able to make the most of the material if they reflect on their own attitudes, strengths and prejudices as part of their work with young people. Ideally this will happen within a framework of professional supervision. Our knowledge and opinions about young people in general, and how we view the significance of factors such as class, 'race' and culture, gender, disability and sexuality will influence how we communicate with each young person.

The power inherent in professional roles has an impact on communication and some workers have to work hard to overcome the connotations of their job or uniform. TSA has other material that helps workers explore their own knowledge and attitudes in relation to working with young people. For example, *Listening in Colour* (created by Youth Access) contains a variety of exercises for individuals to work through, and *Working with Young People* has similarly rich material for trainers to use in group work to develop interpersonal skills.

For a broader exploration of the subject of communication skills see the references at the end of the manual. The remainder of the short discussion here concentrates on four important aspects of communication with young people:

- **Adolescent development**
- **Non-verbal communication (body language)**
- **Active listening skills**
- **Communicating through activities**

Adolescent development

Human development is not just about biology. All aspects of young people's growth are affected by the immediate environment and wider society in which they grow up. Most workers will recognise the tensions in a society that at some levels espouses youth empowerment, yet at another promotes ever more punitive forms of control.

Young people's approach to communicating also tends to change as they grow older. For example, TSA's research for *Getting Through* noted that in the early teens, young people tend to see good communication in terms of getting what they want, or winning. They are also more likely to resort to temper tantrums when things do not go their way than older teenagers. At this end of adolescence, there is also a tendency for communication with friends to focus on practical purposes such as making arrangements.

Older young people saw communication more in terms of establishing a shared understanding than simply getting their way. They are also more able to recognise the reciprocal nature of communication and see their own part in its success or failure. Communication with friends is more likely to revolve around exchanging views and sharing thoughts and experiences with less of the emphasis on the practical matters than at the younger age.

Clearly these distinctions are broad generalisations and individuals will vary a great deal, but it is important to acknowledge young people's skills and understanding will be changing during adolescence and this will impact on communication with them.

Non-verbal communication

Body language is a crucial component of effective communication. Facial expressions and body posture can enhance or undermine welcoming language. Whilst many proponents of active listening suggest facing the other person in an open posture and maintaining eye contact, this can sometimes increase self-consciousness for young people, and, depending on the nature of their role, workers find that it can also be helpful to talk with young people whilst engaged in another activity with them, or whilst travelling somewhere. In these situations, it is still important to have some eye contact and to show that you are focusing properly on what they are saying by using other skills of active listening.

Active listening skills

Active listening techniques include repeating, paraphrasing and summarising key parts of what has been said, and asking open questions. The emphasis is on following the flow and the meaning of what the other person is saying rather than letting your own agenda direct the conversation. Where you have promised to take action, or where the young person has said they will take action, then following this up also shows that you have been listening. Allowing time for the person to express themselves gives them space to reflect on what they are talking about and shows that you are keen on hearing what they have to say, rather than filling the gap with your own opinion.

The fundamental principles of 'getting on the right wavelength' with young people are often demonstrated by those who work effectively with young people with learning and communication difficulties. They learn to tune in to the young person at many levels and be aware of the significance of behavioural changes or changes in tone of voice. They are also creative in finding effective and personalised ways of communicating, and are adaptable at using the most appropriate communication methods and aids with different people. When delivering information, they are usually good at 'chunking it down' into easily manageable pieces, and checking that the young person has understood.

Communicating through activities

If you have the opportunity, activity-based projects, residential weekends, outings and simple everyday things such as cooking, applying make-up, plaiting hair into braids, decorating, shopping, eating out, taking part in sports, or accompanying a young person to a doctor's appointment can provide a chance to relate to young people on a different level. It may be that your role includes such activities on an everyday basis, or they may only happen on 'special' occasions such as outings or residential trips.

Outings and residential weekends are a time when you can see the young people you work with in a different light. Although the setting is away from daily routines, the insights you can get are often to do with the reality of the young person's normal day-to-day existence. You may discover that someone has a bigger problem than you realised with basic independence skills, or that someone else has much more confidence in a different setting or with a new group of people. All these insights can be valuable information as the basis for future work after the outing or residential.

In so far as you might see young people in a different light, they will probably see you that way too. It's a good chance to show a different side of yourself, whilst maintaining professional boundaries and responsibilities.

Sometimes young people find it difficult to talk in formal settings where the conversation is the sole focus of the session. Going on a journey with a young person can be a good opportunity to talk without having to be so formal. Because they don't have to sit facing you when you are driving, they can feel less self conscious about what they are saying. But be prepared for these informal moments to be the times when important disclosures may be made, because the barriers to talking have been lowered a little.

Many young people find it easier to talk in the evening or late at night and again a residential setting allows the opportunity for you to be there if they want to talk to you. Try not to be so busy that you might seem unavailable.

Unusual activities (that is, activities you don't usually do with the young people you work with), allow for the possibility that young people's expertise will outstrip yours and this can be very healthy for your relationship.

Communicating for different purposes

Different roles require different styles of communicating. For instance some workers may be focussed on helping the young person find information, whereas others may be mentoring, or supporting young people to mentor each other. Within your specific role, you also change the way you communicate according to the context. For example, if you are meeting with a young person for a discussion on some issue, you may have pre-arranged a time and some privacy for your meeting. If the young person finds it hard to talk, you will probably use active listening skills with open questions and lots of encouragement, to help them say what is on their mind. However, if a young person passes you in the corridor and wants to talk when you are unable to, you are more likely to use closed questions, such as, 'Could you come and talk to me after the next lesson?' than open questions that encourage more talking. You can still show your willingness to listen by means of a simple empathic statement like, 'I can see this is important but I can't stop right now. Can we talk later?' but you will be using skills that limit conversation rather than open it up.

Although workers need to use different communication approaches for different purposes, communication should always be underpinned by an attitude of respect, honesty, acceptance of where young people are at and a belief that change is possible. It is also helpful to bear in mind the long term view of helping young people develop their own skills and values for the future, rather than focusing solely on sorting out immediate problems for them.

This section starts by looking at creating a welcoming environment and also beginning and ending relationships. It then outlines some of the skills involved in communicating for different purposes. In the section *Further Resources and Suppliers* at the end of this book, you will find references to books that describe these skills more fully. The different purposes grouped here are:

> **Establishing a relationship and understanding the issues**
>
> **Giving information**
>
> **Making referrals**
>
> **Supporting peer-led projects and participation work**
>
> **Confronting and challenging negative patterns and behaviours**
>
> **Encouraging and motivating for change**

Creating a welcoming environment

It may not be up to you to design the place you work in. For example, some outreach workers meet young people in the places they hang out. Other workers make home visits, or a youth worker may see a group in a classroom used by many different groups for different purposes.

If you work in a specific place, or run a centre used by young people, you will have more opportunity to think about what makes this place attractive and comfortable for a wide range of young people. Consulting with them and involving them in the design is the best way of finding this out and helping them to feel ownership of the place.

Here are some questions to consider:

- Are there areas for private conversations?
- Is the entrance clearly signed but not too prominent (easy to slip in and out of unnoticed)?
- How clean and cared for does it look?
- How big or small is it and does this suit its function?
- Is there any graffiti? Is this deliberate?
- What is on the walls? Are posters and notices inclusive to all groups?
- Are the lighting and heating adequate and appropriate?
- Is there any music? Who chooses it?
- What kind of furniture is there? Who chooses or paints it?
- What kind of messages does the environment give to young people?
- How safe is it? What would happen if there was a fire or a fight?
- What kind of people go there and what kind of atmosphere is created?
- What makes it welcoming or unwelcoming?
- What would your first impressions be if you were a young person looking for support?
- How welcoming is the environment to:
    - a young person who uses a wheelchair?
    - a young person from a minority ethnic group?
    - a young person with learning difficulties?
    - a young person who has a hearing or visual impairment?
    - a young lesbian, gay, bisexual or transexual person?
- In what ways are young people likely to have heard about the place? Does this information reach all young people equally?

If you work in different places where the young people go, show that you respect their space, whilst doing your best to create an atmosphere that is safe and welcoming. You should also be able to create an opportunity for privacy if needed.

Communication strategies for beginnings and endings

Any piece of work with an individual or group has a beginning and an end. The work may be a one-off or drop-in session, a time-limited issue-based group or series of individual sessions, an ongoing group or an open-ended piece of individual work, but at some point each of these begins and comes to a close. Even within ongoing work, there is a beginning and an end to each session. Beginnings and endings are particularly significant for many people and may raise anxieties that are connected with previous changes and losses in their lives. For this reason it is important to be aware of how you handle beginnings and endings yourself, and how you negotiate them with the young people you work with. Because young people generally live their lives with more immediacy than adults, and change can happen very quickly for them, it is as well to make sure that each session you have with them has a sense of completion, even if it is part of ongoing work. In this way, if the young person does not come back for any reason, they will have had the benefit of a completed session, where issues have been clarified and positive feedback has been given to them.

When you start to work with a new individual or group, both sides will be engaged with the question, 'Will I be able to work with this person?' Observation will be going on at all levels. The way you dress, speak and behave will communicate something about you to the young person or people you are with, and you will be forming an opinion of them in the same way. Beginnings are often affected by the following questions:

- how and why did the referral come about?
- who made the referral?
- does the referrer have any further influence over the process and outcomes of the work, or any right to know what goes on in the sessions?
- does the young person feel he has a choice about being there?
- has she been fully informed about your role?
- have you been given any information about her?
- what impression have you already formed on the basis of this information?

It is important to clarify these issues openly with the young person or group of people at the start of your work together and establish the extent to which their involvement is voluntary.

At the beginning of working together, relationship issues between you will be very important, but it is also useful to get an idea of the aims of the young people, in relation to the content of the work you are to do together. You should let them know any aims you have too. Along with the aims, it is useful to find out what sort of thing might stop the young person achieving what they hope to achieve. What are their fears about this work? What sort of things might they do to sabotage their own progress? You can find out some answers to these questions by sensitive and collaborative discussion.

In group work, this initial discussion may lead to a group contract, or ground rules for the group. These rules are the things that make the group's aims or expectations more possible and the things they fear less likely to happen or easier to handle when they do. Ground rules are usually a set of agreed statements devised by the group about the way they intend to conduct themselves. Generally group contracts should include anti-discriminatory statements and a statement that clarifies the level of confidentiality that can be maintained. Each group member should have a copy of the ground rules and they should be displayed during group sessions so they can be referred to at any time. For instance if someone does something that contravenes the rules, anyone can challenge them. At the end of the group's work together, they should refer back to their original expectations and fears, to check how well they managed to achieve their expectations and whether their fears were realised or confronted.

With individuals, there may or may not be a need for a formal contract, depending on the context of your work, but you will still need to discuss the purpose of your time together, and how you are likely to be best able to achieve this purpose. Again, it will be useful to have some sort of record of this, so the young person can look back at the end and assess what he or she has achieved.

During this introductory discussion, the worker should make it very clear what their own role is and whether there is a set time-limit on the work. If there is not, it is important that both sides know from the start how it will be decided that the work has finished, and what choice the young person has in this decision. Workers should remember that, although they are aiming to engage well with young people, their aim should be to empower them, rather than to make them dependent on the worker. Being clear and supportive about endings can help the young person to move on with confidence.

Endings can come about in different ways. A time-limit may have been reached; a young person may have decided not to return for the next planned session; a sudden change in circumstances may have brought about a premature ending; a worker may be handing on, or referring the young person to someone else. Sometimes the ending is not the one you expected or planned, but as far as possible, try to make sure the following elements are part of the ending:

* evaluating the outcomes of the work against the young people's initial hopes and aims

* summarising and clarifying what has gone on

* itemising any action to be taken by you or the young people before the next session

* making sure the young person has all the information they need relating to any referral you have made, or that they have been introduced to the next person they will be working with

* affirming the strengths and positive qualities of the young person and making sure they know where and how to find other resources

If these elements are built in to each session to some degree, the young person will potentially benefit from them even if they do not return for future planned sessions.

There are many creative ways of conducting evaluations with groups or individuals. They involve looking back to see what worked and didn't work, what was enjoyed or not. The group or individual reflect on their own learning, and give feedback to each other and to the worker. The worker gives feedback to them as well, including details of the strengths he has observed. Any party or celebration you hold to mark the end of the work should take place after the evaluation has been completed.

Within each session, certain patterns may develop around the beginning and end, and these can create a feeling of safety for the group or individual. For instance, you might have a bin into which people throw the thoughts they are happy to get rid of at the start of a session. In group work, make sure the binned thoughts are labelled because at the end group members might want them back. In a group, ice-breaker activities and warm-ups are often used to create a formal structure for the beginning of the group session. In individual work, it may be that the session usually starts with the same sort of questions, statements or chat. This can be helpful because the familiarity of the pattern not only creates safety, but helps the worker to notice when something is different, which could signal a change in the young person's circumstances, mood or outlook.

Similarly at the end of the session, a familiar pattern may make it easier for a young person to register the end of the work and prepare themselves for whatever they are going on to next. Aim to start and finish sessions on time.

Example

> In a unit for vulnerable young people, each day starts in small groups, with a chat about where they're at, timetables for the day, and anything else they want to talk about. At the end of the day, they gather together after their various activities for another twenty minute chat to sum up the day, talk about things that have come up, and look ahead to the following day.

Establishing a relationship and understanding the issues

Whatever your role in connection with young people, you will need to engage with them and establish some sort of relationship, however brief. As you get to know them, you will also learn something about their way of experiencing the world. Many young people complain that adults don't really listen to them or try to understand the world from their point of view. If you work exclusively with groups, the relationship you establish with the group will be different from the relationships you might establish with individual group members, but it is still helpful to get to know the world through the viewpoint of those you work with. The communication skills that are helpful for making relationships with young people and understanding their issues are ones that you are likely to employ throughout your work. Underlying these skills are the values of empathy, openness and acceptance. Acceptance means that you accept and value the young person, even if you don't like their behaviour.

Communication skills for establishing a relationship and understanding the issues

- Giving undivided attention to the other person. You can give them your attention while you are engaged on an activity with them, and many young people would prefer to communicate in this way than by sitting face to face. Giving full attention means you're not thinking of other things or wondering how you can drive home your own agenda or finish the other person's sentence. It shows the young person that you value them.

- Showing your attentiveness in non-verbal ways. This means having some eye contact, though it doesn't have to be constant. It also means making encouraging gestures and having an open posture.

- Observing the young person through all your senses. Again, this doesn't indicate an overpowering intensity – it just means you need to develop an awareness of the idiosyncrasies of the young person. If you develop this sense, you are more likely to pick up changes of mood, or sense when something is not right.

- Being open and honest. Try not to hide behind a professional mask. Young people appreciate workers being themselves, even though they have to keep to professional boundaries. Let them in on some of your personal interests, share a joke or a moment of frustration. But be careful not to overpower a young person with your personality, your anecdotes and your zany sense of humour.

- Show that you have heard what young people say by paraphrasing or summarising what they have said: 'Let me make sure I've got that right…' 'So are you saying…'

- Ask open-ended questions (ones that require a response that's more than a single word or phrase) such as: 'What worked best when you tried it before?' Put aside your assumptions and be prepared for unexpected responses.

- Try to read between the lines to understand the message behind the factual information. Check out whether you've got it right: 'It sounds like you've had enough of that situation. Am I right?'

- Try to avoid doing all the talking yourself, or telling the young person what to do or say when they haven't asked for your advice. Follow the young person's lead with an open, enquiring mind.

- If you are working with a group, you will be focusing on what helps the group to work together, and what issues they want to work on, rather than on individuals, at least initially, but you can still use the same skills of demonstrating your full attention, feeding back to the group what they say and do and asking open questions. Over time you are likely to develop individual relationships with the group members as well as your relationship with the group as a whole.

Tip

Some young people might be very wary of adults trying to get to know and understand them. Make sure they are in control of whatever makes the situation safe for them. They may want to sit near the door or have the door open. There's no reason they should trust you, even when they get to know you – they may feel they've been caught out like that before.

Giving Information

Information is power. The way we share or withhold information gives us more or less power over others, whether we want that power or not. Workers can help young people to feel in control of their lives by facilitating their access to useful information. For some workers, giving information is their main function and this role will be well defined within their organisation's policies. Other workers give young people different types of information on a less formal basis.

Communication skills for giving information

- Giving information is not the same as giving advice. Present information in a way that is not biased or leading. If you want to give advice or guidance, or if that is the nature of your service, be clear that is what you are doing.

- Having access to information is empowering. Can you assist the young person to access the information they need themselves?

- Information in the form of instructions should be simply stated, one step at a time. Check that the young person understands by asking them to repeat the instructions in their own words. Give the instructions in more than one way if you can (for example using words and diagrams or pictures, or give a demonstration).

- If the young person needs to remember the instructions for another time, give them a written or illustrated copy.

- If the information you are giving is personal, ask what the young person wants to do with it. Do they want to take it away or leave it with you?

- Make sure the young person has and understands all the information they need. Does anyone connected to them need this information as well?

- Make sure the young person knows that it's up to them what they do with the information you give them, if that is the case. Otherwise tell them who else has been given the information and why.

Tip

If the information you give the young person is in the form of bad news, try to establish that someone is around for them, or that someone can be with them when you see them, if that's appropriate. Remember that they may be shocked and unlikely to remember much of what you say. Keep your message simple and make sure you give them your details so they can get back to you later for more information. Give them some information in written form if that's appropriate. Make sure that their immediate physical needs are taken care of, especially if they show signs of being in shock. Express your acknowledgement of their response, without making assumptions about how they feel. Don't leave them alone without finding out what they are going to do next and who will be with them. Stay with them if you can. They may respond in ways that seem inappropriate to you. Don't criticise their response.

Making referrals

Some of the key issues about making referrals are to do with choice and privacy – who decides to make the referral and how much information is passed on? Usually these issues are governed by policies in your work place, according to the type of referral you are likely to make. Ideally, the choice to be referred elsewhere should belong to the young person, who should be fully informed of the options. However, if you are carrying out child protection procedures you will be expected to follow a system for referring information on to another person or organisation. Whether or not the referral is in the control of the young person, the young person's choices and their privacy should still be a prime concern and the requirements of the law should be fully explained.

Communication skills for making referrals

- Regularly update your own information about policies, practices and local organisations.

- Network with other services and workers, both within and outside your own organisation, so you can make referrals on the basis of personal contact.

- Make clear to the young person from the start if there are limits on their choice about referrals, for example within child protection policies. Explain the limits of confidentiality at the start of your work together.

- If you want to make a referral because of someone else's superior knowledge or expertise, or because another organisation has a particular specialism, explain clearly to the young person what this other person has to offer. Show them any printed or website information you have. Ask if they would be interested in a referral. If not, discuss the alternatives.

- Discuss with them the options for making the referral, for example they may make their own approach, you may make an appointment for them, or you may do it together. If they wish, you may be able to take them there.

- Explain clearly what information, if any, you will pass on and who will have access to this. Ideally the young person should decide what information is passed on.

- Answer their questions and look out for anxieties they may have.

- If necessary, rehearse what might happen when they go to the other organisation. Remember that young people may be a lot more nervous than they seem about encountering new situations in strange surroundings.

- Be clear about who else, if anyone, is aware of the referral.

- If this referral ends your own involvement, make that clear.

- Check that the young person has understood what has gone on between you and can say it back in their own words.

If you are the first-contact person for your organisation, make sure the young person understands your role and that you are not the person they will be seeing in the future. Don't encourage them to tell you more about themselves than they need to.

If another organisation or person has more appropriate expertise or knowledge, express this positively (tell them how your colleague can help) rather than negatively (I can't help you with that).

Supporting peer led projects and participation work

Peer led projects include peer mediation, peer support work and peer education. Participation work is the process of involving young people in decision-making. What workers in these two areas have in common is that their role is not a leadership one, but more that of facilitators. Workers who support peer led projects and participation work don't abdicate their responsibility but they encourage young people to negotiate for what they want and they equip them with skills that many people used to consider the province solely of adults.

Communication skills for peer led projects and participation work

*   Working with young people to advertise the project in an inclusive way, so no-one experiences an unnecessary barrier to joining.

*   Interviewing and recruiting volunteers. Involve young people in this process. The care that is taken at this stage communicates to young people the value of the project.

*   Training young people in new skills, such as listening and interviewing.

*   Awareness training for managers and decision-makers. If they don't really understand what is needed from them in the way of action, feedback and extra resources, then there's not much point involving young people in decision-making. Awareness training for managers is generally harder to get off the ground than a participation project itself.

*   Supervising peer educators, mediation and support workers. Again, these projects should not be set up in order to save money. They should be for the benefit of all the young people involved and the resources should include substantial training and supervision programmes if the projects are to work well. The skills gained by peer workers can sometimes be formally recognised through qualifications.

*   Group facilitation. This includes making groupwork lively and fun. A lively, interesting looking group can be one of the main incentives for young people getting involved.

- Modelling an openness to learning. These projects are likely to be fairly new. The worker's enthusiasm for learning from a new situation can influence the young people in the group. It's a great opportunity to show that mistakes are okay and are a good resource for learning.

- Preparing groups of young people for official meetings. This involves clarifying and making copies of information in suitable formats, and rehearsing questions and feedback on reports. If the meeting is planned by others, try to go through agendas and procedures with the young people beforehand.

- Translating wordy official documents into shorter, more accessible handouts, for example in preparation for young people's meetings with council decision-makers.

- Sharing information about the project with colleagues and negotiating their involvement. These projects usually have implications for others working in an organisation, or for workers in other organisations.

Tip

Consider the ways in which decisions are taken within your participation group and your organisation generally. What are the pros and cons of various democratic processes? Are there other ways of doing things?

Confronting and challenging negative patterns and behaviours

Challenging negative patterns and behaviours is important in both group and individual work. It is preferable to know the young person a while before you confront them with these patterns or behaviour, as they are more likely to listen if you already have an effective working relationship. Also, you will be able to frame your challenge within a general statement about their progress, which also contains some positive comments. Get to know your own style of communication and practice assertiveness. Some people are better at challenging than others. But most of us know, deep down, when it's necessary.

Communication skills for confronting and challenging negative patterns and behaviours

- Giving feedback. Make your feedback an observation of the young person's behaviour, not an attack on their personality, for example, 'I notice that you have been acting very aggressively towards your friends recently.' Present it as an 'I' statement, rather than a statement of fact: 'I feel disappointed when I hear that you've been shoplifting again' rather than 'You're a regular little thief aren't you?' If you want the young person to make a change, state precisely what it is: 'I'd like you to arrive on time for this session tomorrow. Thank you.'

- Restricting feedback to what is useful for the young person. Deal with one issue at a time but stick with it and follow through with any monitoring of this behaviour that you negotiate with the young person.

- Including a positive message whilst remaining truthful. For example: 'I thought your art work in the group was very impressive, but I was angry that you ripped Jodie's painting on your way out and I want you to apologise to her.'

- Challenging group members who are dominating a group. If they are very vocal and offer lots of opinions, thank them for their expertise and ask if they can think of ways to help everyone in the group have a say.

- Confronting racism, sexism and other forms of oppression by referring to the group or individual contract, which should include statements about inflammatory remarks. It's not always easy to do this, when you're just beginning to make headway with the perpetrator, but it is an indication that you keep to your word and that you have respect for people. Keep your challenge non-personal.

- Challenging with a light touch. When a behaviour needs to be challenged, it's not always most productive to make a big issue out of it. You can comment on the behaviour to show that it hasn't escaped you, followed by: 'But today is supposed to be about having fun' and move on. This approach is often the best one to use with someone who is likely to become very defensive when challenged. This is not to say that they should escape the consequences of serious negative behaviours. It's a question of timing, and sometimes giving someone the opportunity to rectify something on their own. But if something needs commenting on, don't ignore it.

- Raising awareness about negative self-beliefs; 'I keep hearing you call yourself crap. That's not how I see you and it puzzles me that you see yourself that way.' Once you have pointed out a particular negative self-belief, the young person can't help but be aware of it, and question why they believe it. You can help them to think of an alternative positive statement that they can say to themselves whenever they find themselves about to use the negative one.

- Teaching thought-stopping techniques for negative thought patterns. Some young people use a rubber band on their wrist which they snap and say 'Stop' whenever the negative beliefs kick in. Many people talk to themselves in a negative or punitive way at some point and it can be a useful topic for work in a group.

Tip

Some workers are in roles where control and discipline are prominent features. Most young people can differentiate between someone who maintains the necessary discipline by 'asking nicely' and someone who exerts their power because they enjoy it.

Encouraging and motivating for change

In order for a worker to work on change with a young person, the young person needs to be actively involved. So for a start they need to acknowledge the need for change. Sometimes this happens alongside particular sets of circumstances. For example, they might be outgrowing particular habits just when something or somebody forces them to question why they are doing it. If this happens when their life is reasonably stable and there is some support around for them, they stand a good chance of success in making the change they want. Workers can potentially be both the person who makes them question why they are doing it, and the one who provides support while they make the change.

Communication skills for encouraging and motivating change

- Offering new perspectives. This is a form of challenge - it challenges old perspectives! For example, a person sees themselves and describes themselves in a particular way, but their behaviour says something different. A worker can offer the young person a 'new perspective' by questioning this difference between one reality and the other: 'You're such a good football player and I know you want to take that seriously, but I've seen the effect your heavy smoking has on you, when you get on the pitch.'

- Praising. Some young people don't like being praised in front of their friends, so you need to be careful about this. Praise is most effective when it's very specific. 'Global' praise such as 'You're such a wonderful person' is hard to believe, but something specific such as, 'You made a very thought-provoking presentation to the class' is more believable.

- Using solution-focused questions. These are usually very specific and help the person to focus on the result they want to get: 'What would your life be like right now if this change were to happen?' 'Tell me about the times when this doesn't happen? – what's different about those times?' 'What would you have to do to make this happen?'

- Helping the young person to look at the obstacles and resources associated with this change. Which of the resources can they use to help themselves overcome the obstacles? What resources and obstacles are in their own heads, or a result of past experience, and which are 'out there'?

- Self-disclosure. If prompted, it can be helpful if the worker talks about a change they made that was difficult.

- Normalising and rehearsing the possibility of failure. What might cause this? What could the young person do to deal with failure? What would be their first step?

- Helping the young person to identify other people, resources and organisations to support this change.

Tip

Scaling can be a helpful technique towards change. The young person gives their change a number (1-10) on a scale of 'do-ability'. Ask them what could move this number up the scale? Is this something they can make happen? What's in the way? After identifying some first steps, ask them to assess the 'do-ability' of their change again.

Part Two

Creating and adapting your own resources

Creating and adapting your own resources

We all have our own ways of communicating. Your style of working needs to be adaptable enough to suit the many ways people learn.

- Some of us are better when we sit down with pen and paper, or at the computer screen and put things down in words. It helps us clear our heads and gives us something to keep and refer to later.

- Others like to doodle and draw, colour things in, fill in bubbles and clouds with words or images. We respond well to visual metaphors – a picture of a crossroads or a window can help us to think about our future plans.

- Some of us can barely sit still when we're working – we need to pace around, handle things, see our ideas pinned up on the wall where we can rearrange them into a different order, stand the coffee cups on the table to represent the projects we're working on.

- Some people like to act things out. They retell their experiences with embellishments and rehearse what they're going to say and do in advance.

- Some people work best when they're listening to music and some don't.

- Some like clear instructions, some just want to throw themselves in and learn by doing. Some let things mull over for a long time and look at things from all angles, while others like to read all the information they can get. Some people really don't get the idea until they've had some examples or case studies to think about. Some like discussion and others like to dance.

Fortunately most people can work in several different styles and are happy as long as they can communicate through at least one of their favoured styles. This applies both to you and the young people you work with. In this handbook there are examples of many different activities that can achieve the same purpose through different communication media. This is to help you use your own creativity to recognise a number of different options for approaching any task or topic with young people, and adapt your approach so it suits the young people you are working with.

Your resources and activities also need to be accessible to young people with a variety of special needs and your creativity will be engaged in adapting your approach to suit those with sensory, communicative or mobility impairments, learning and behavioural difficulties, language needs and cultural differences.

The activities described in this section are grouped according to five different communication approaches: the written word, visuals, moving sorting and handling, drama and activities.

Example

A substance abuse worker has used a 'matching sentences' individual worksheet activity for months with different groups, as a way of delivering certain information. As an alternative, she pastes each half of each sentence onto card and sticks the cards on the backs of group members. Now they have to mingle round until they find their matching partners. This seems to engage more young people more fully than her previous approach. The next time she delivers similar information, she will try splitting the group into teams and running the 'matching sentences' task as a race between teams.

The remainder of Part Two consists of examples of activities for communicating with young people. We have grouped the activities into five sections, reflecting different styles of engaging young people in learning:

Communicating through the written word
(including reading, writing and word games) p.33

Communicating through visuals
(including drawing, watching television and mapping) p.57

Communicating through moving, sorting and handling
(including dot voting, continuum lines and symbolic objects) p.85

Communicating through drama
(including forum theatre, role play and non-verbal language) p.109

Practice them, adapt, mix and match and above all create...

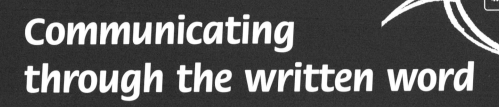

Communicating through the written word

Written word activities suit many young people but those who have difficulties with reading and spelling may experience these activities as a confirmation of their failure. Less open-ended options are easier than those that rely on lots of 'free' writing. For example in 'Making Lists' there is a suggestion that you could prepare some lists in advance so a young person has the option of highlighting items of interest to talk about rather than creating their own written list from scratch. However, don't assume that someone who has spelling problems won't want to write. They may be just as keen as the next person to keep a journal or write a song if they know they're not going to be judged on their spelling. Symbols can be used to replace words in some of these activities, for those who use symbols to communicate. You should also find out if any of the young people you are working with need special lighting or positioning, or special technology to deal with the written word. For those who don't relate well to the written word, consider how you could adapt the activities to other types of activity.

Contents

Writing the guide book

Writing the guidebook' can help young people to take a fresh perspective on a situation or relationship. It puts them in the powerful role of researcher and expert on the situation.

Examples

→ A small group of young people whose relationships have recently ended decide to use what they have learnt to write **Surviving the break–up: a guide to getting over a relationship**.

→ A young man who is about to include step-siblings in his newly blended family writes about this in his journal under the heading, **A rough guide to getting along with my family** This helps him to take a fresh look at some of the difficulties he is going through and see some of the strengths in the situation as well as the problems.

→ A group of students research and write **A guidebook to getting through exams** for their own benefit and that of other students.

The way it works

The guidebook approach lends itself to consultation. Young people may devise a set of questions on the topic and decide who they will interview to get a range of opinions and ideas (for example on how to survive a break-up or how to get through exams). When all information has been gathered, they sort and present it under clear headings.

Guidebooks can also be used in individual work, to help a young person distance themselves from a problematic situation, and see it from different perspectives. For example, **A rough guide to getting along with my family** could start from questions such as:

- If you were to swap places with a complete stranger of your own age, what rules would they need to learn quickly in order to get on with everyone in your family?

- What helps things to go well between people in your family? What makes things go wrong?

- How do people in your family make up with each other after an argument?

This sort of guidebook can be used to explore the potential for change, as young people notice and build on positive factors as well as seeing the pitfalls. Being encouraged to find patterns and unspoken rules in a situation can also help them to gain perspective and take things less personally.

Tips for using it:

- The point can be made just as well with humour. Encourage any humorous approaches that develop.

- Encourage art work – cartoons, drawings, photos, clip art.

- Think about the audience – who will read the guidebook, or is it for personal use?

- Bring in other guidebooks as examples – travel guides, how-to books, self-help books.

Other things you can do with it

- Young people can make guidebooks as part of a peer mentoring project, such as older pupils helping younger pupils to settle in to a new school.

Making lists

Making lists can be a way of triggering discussion on a topic, generating ideas towards action or summing up a session's work. A young person could also use lists to express brief thoughts on a topic in their journal. Lists with headings such as 'Three things I would do if …' encourage a fast, spontaneous response. This is a format often found in young people's magazines and websites.

Examples

 In her journal, a young woman fills in the following lists:

1. If I ruled the world... Name three things you would do
2. If I could have three things I wanted right now … What would they be?
3. If I could be somewhere else right now… Where would you most like to be?
4. If I could have any job or career I wanted... What would you most like to do?

 As a 'getting to know you' warm-up activity with a new group, the facilitator has prepared some cards, and on each he has written a request. Each request is to name a 'list of three.' He gives these cards out to the group. They mingle around and find a partner. Each person asks the other the question that is on their card, and waits for a reply. When both sides have finished they swap cards and move on to someone else. The type of questions on the cards are:

1. name three things that get you down…
2. name three people or things that cheer you up…
3. name three things that calm you down…
4. name three things that make you laugh…
5. name three of your favourite smells…

The way it works

Present a set of headings on a topic, as in the examples above. Young people can write the lists or talk them through. Young people may fill in lists to express their current state of mind in a journal (see **Journals and Logs** in this section).

see page 54
MORE IDEAS

Tips for using it:

- Keep headings or questions short and clear.
- Limit the number of headings.
- Use lively language (check out teen magazines and websites).
- Make clear spaces for the young person to write in.
- Don't include questions that encourage young people to share personal information in unsafe situations. For large group activities, keep it light.
- Try out suggestions for yourself first to see how it feels, before asking young people to give this information.
- Respect the diversity of young people's lives (for example, don't automatically refer to 'your mum and dad').
- Experiment with different kinds of typeface (fonts), clip art and drawings.
- Use coloured paper.
- Young people may like to create their own list formats on a topic, and try them out on others.

Other things you can do with it

Prepare a ready-made list under a topic heading. Give the young person a highlighter pen and invite them to pick out the items that interest them. For example:

> ### Things to do in September
>
> pack my school bag the night before – wear something I wouldn't usually wear – talk to an animal – save some money – eat something I wouldn't usually eat – walk away from an argument – change my hairstyle – get up early – stop smoking – go for a run – paint a picture – recycle something – go for a swim – sing a song – write a song – watch a tv programme someone else wants to watch – find out more about someone in my class – stand up to a bully – have a lie-in – learn to count to ten in another language

- Print suggestions such as the ones above on separate pieces of card. Ask the young person to choose five, either randomly or deliberately, and talk to you about them.

- With the young person's permission, date and keep lists that deal with feelings, behaviours, attitudes and current situations, and refer back to them together later to monitor personal change.

Quizzes and questionnaires

Quizzes are a prominent and popular feature of young people's magazines. They are a useful way of checking information on a topic, either at the start of work or for evaluating learning at the end. They can also be used as a light-hearted way of exploring attitudes and personal characteristics. Questionnaires are a useful way of gathering a range of opinions and information from other people.

Examples

 A week after an information session on a topic, the facilitator holds a 'quiz night', with the group arranged into teams. A small prize is given to the winning team.

 A group devise a questionnaire to gather views on school transport.

The way it works

Quizzes can be created with multiple choice answers, true or false options, or with no clues at all. Multiple choice answers increase the chances of success. Quizzes can be devised by the group leader, or the group can be divided into two, with each team creating a quiz for the other. At the beginning of a topic, a quiz can be created by gathering all the questions on this topic into a hat. Write the questions up, and then distribute them to different pairs or groups. Give them good sources of information and ask them to come back to the next session with the quiz answers. For 'personality' quizzes, show examples from teen magazines and websites, and ask the young people or person to devise their own on a particular topic, such as 'What makes a good friend?'

Questionnaires can be used to consult with people who use a particular facility or are affected by a certain issue. The young people must consider who they are going to question, what they want to know, and how they will compare and present the results. Questionnaires need to be planned carefully so that the range of opinions represents all groups affected or involved in the issue. Young people should avoid using leading questions or letting their own bias affect the choice of questions.

Tips for using it:

- Keep these activities light and fun. They are not meant to be like exams, nor to make anyone feel a failure.

- Quiz questions and answers can be livened up by appropriate presentation. For instance, cardbord cut-outs of bottles could have a question about alcohol on the front with answers and information on the back.

- Before use, questionnaires should be piloted with a small group who will give feedback on the questions.

Other things you can do with it

- Devise a quiz with single word answers. Arrange these answers into a word search square.

- Put individual questions and answers on separate cards. Using two groups of young people, give each group a complete but jumbled set of cards and see which group can match the right sets of questions and answers first (see **Matching Sentences** in this section).

see page 46 MORE IDEAS

Charters and bills of rights

Charters and bills of rights both convey a sense of reforming a situation that is experienced as oppressive, discriminatory and unfair. This may be because of ongoing prejudice in society or the community, or because past experiences have led a young person to feel they have no rights and little value. Charters and bills are useful tools for work on assertiveness, and for work with minority groups who experience infringements of their rights. The creation of a group charter can help a group define what it is about and what it aims to address. Work on a bill of rights may focus on factors affecting a specific area, such as sexual health.

Examples

 A group of young wheelchair users create a 'wheeled charter' that expresses their expectations for full access to a public facility.

 A worker helps a vulnerable young man to create his own bill of rights to sexual health.

The way it works

The first step towards young people negotiating rights with others, is recognising that they have them. In groups, or with individuals, start from general discussion about human rights and topical examples of how some people's rights are abused. Focus in on their own world and ask them to list the rights they would like to enjoy on a daily basis. These can include the right to have certain opinions and feelings, the right to access information, support and protection, the right to say 'no' and so on. These lists can be created on an individual basis or in small groups. When lists are completed, open up discussion about which rights are easy or difficult to claim. Some rights may compete with the rights of others. Workers should be clear about what is and is not up for negotiation and why. When the charters and bills are written, help young people to identify an action they could take, alone or together to stand up for one or more of these rights.

Tips for using it

- Introduce relevant information about rights, such as Article 12 of the United Nations Convention on the Rights of the Child, along with Articles 2,3 and 23.

- Introduce up to date information about legal rights at different ages.

- When a charter or bill of rights has been agreed, negotiate where it will be kept and how it will be used.

- Creating charters and bills raises awareness about equality issues. Take care to work with young people to the point where they are empowered to change something that affects them, rather than raising awareness of inequality and doing nothing about it.

- Be careful not to imply that young people's experience of oppression, or their lack of assertiveness is their fault.

- Acknowledge the inequalities of the world we live in.

- Consider the idea of responsibilities alongside the notion of rights.

Other things you can do with it

- Use scenario card activities to identify situations where rights are being abused, and generate ideas about how to confront this abuse (see **Scenario Cards** in this section).

see page 50 MORE IDEAS

see page 110 MORE IDEAS

- Use forum theatre to dramatise decisions over personal rights (see **Forum Theatre** in the section on drama).

- Many young people enjoy watching dramas about people in prison. They often identify with the feeling of being an underdog. Watch an episode from a prison series as a starting point for discussion (see **Watching Television** in the section on visuals).

see page 76 MORE IDEAS

- Use a moving circles activity to explore situations where the rights of one person or group are in conflict with those of another person or group (see **Moving Circles** in the section on moving, sorting and handling).

see page 92 MORE IDEAS

Quick thoughts

At the start of a new topic, these are useful for generating lots of ideas or getting an indication how much the group or individual already knows on the topic. They are also a way of encouraging an input from everyone as no-one can be 'wrong.' Quick thoughts can generate some interesting new angles on a topic.

Examples

→ *A discussion on bullying begins with the question, 'How many kinds of bullying can you think of?' The group writes down all the responses they can come up with until they have filled a flip-chart sheet.*

→ *At the start of a video-making project, the facilitator asks, 'What are all the things we need to think about before we start?' She charts the group's responses and uses this as a starting point for planning.*

→ *In individual work, a young person who is often absent from school fills a sheet of paper as quickly as possible with his quick thoughts on the topic 'Staying away from school.'*

The way it works

Quick thoughts can be collected in different ways:

- The group leader, or an appointed person who is a fast writer, writes down all suggestions, uncensored, on a flip chart.

see page 104
MORE IDEAS

- Each person has a set of large sticky notes. They are given a few minutes to write one suggestion per note, and then at the same time, everyone sticks their suggestions up on the board in any order (see **Dot Voting** in the section on moving, sorting and handling for further development of this idea).

If you are working with an individual, you can take their initial list and ask them to choose which idea they'd like to talk about or do some work on. Or ask them if they noticed any particular feelings as they wrote this list.

5

Tips for using it:

- Write exactly what is said with no censoring or modifying initially.

- Set a pre-arranged limit, such as 'two minutes' or 'one piece of paper' and stick to it.

- Use phrases like 'thoughts off the top of your head' or 'the first thing you think of' to encourage spontaneity.

Other things you can do with it

- Ask a quick thoughts type question in the middle of a session as an energiser if the session feels stuck.

- Use 'quick thoughts' in the opposite way from what is usually expected. In the middle of a session, if attention is wandering, ask everyone to say one word each in quick succession. The word can be anything that comes to mind as long as it has no connection at all with the topic in question. Participants can challenge each other. If someone can prove that a word is connected to the topic, the person who said that word is out. But if the challenger is wrong, they are out. Quicken the pace and see how quickly you can reduce the number of players in the game to one.

- Small groups can develop quick thoughts simultaneously on different aspects of the same topic.

- Quick thoughts can be structured but still spontaneous and uncensored, as in **Gingerbread Shapes** (see the section on visuals).

see page 74
MORE IDEAS

Ideas exhibition

This is a more in-depth version of quick thoughts and is designed to give everyone the opportunity to develop further their ideas about different aspects of the topic under discussion.

Examples

 A group working on community safety creates an ideas exhibition using three separate questions as their headings: What would make this community safer for teenagers? For small children? For older people?

 A group of young people with learning difficulties is evaluating a residential activity weekend. Photos representing different elements of the weekend are stuck onto blank posters. The young people are invited to write, draw or symbolise their comments on each element.

The way it works

Divide the group into smaller groups, for example A, B and C. Give each group a different question related to the main topic, a piece of flip chart paper and marker pens. The group jot down their responses to their question. After a short time, collect the flip chart sheets and pin them up. This is the exhibition. Give each group a set of sticky dots in red, green and yellow. Ask group A to move to flip chart B, B to C and so on. Each group reads through the ideas of the other group, indicating with a green dot if they agree with a point, a red dot if they disagree and a yellow dot if they want to question it. Then they add their own ideas, but only if they have something to say that hasn't already been said. At an agreed signal, they move on to the next flipchart and do the same, and so on. When the groups have all been round each flip chart, reverse the order of viewing, so they can view, but not add to, the final version of each flipchart until they reach their own. Allow time for the people who put red or yellow dots to voice their disagreements or ask questions of the original writers (see also **Dot Voting** in the section on moving, sorting and handling).

(see page 104 MORE IDEAS)

Tips for using it:

- Don't allow too long for each stage of this activity. There should be scope for each group to add ideas to the previous list. But remember that as each group goes round, there will be more ideas on each chart to comment on before they can start adding their own.

- The final viewing in reverse order is just a chance to quickly see what has been added to each chart since each group had their turn.

Other things you can do with it

- Instead of different questions, you could use the same question, but ask each group to answer from a different viewpoint, such as a young person, a parent or carer, a teacher.

- You can adapt this for individual work. For example, if you are working with someone who has a very negative self-image, ask them to name two good friends or relatives who like them (make sure they will be able to do so first). Pin up two sheets with one of these names on each sheet. Each time the young person makes a negative comment about themselves, ask them what either of these two people would say about them that was more positive. Write it on the relevant sheet and repeat it. At the end of the session, ask the young person to read these positive comments aloud (see **Confronting and Challenging Negative Patterns and Behaviours** in the section on communicating for different purposes).

see page 24 MORE IDEAS

Matching sentences

These activities are useful for helping young people to learn new information or new ways of talking about an issue. Although these are grouped here as a written word style, they lend themselves very easily to moving, sorting and handling activities too.

Examples

➤ During a session aimed to increase emotional literacy, the facilitator gives out worksheets divided into four columns labelled 'angry' 'sad' 'happy' and 'scared.' He then gives out a second sheet of words and phrases that describe these feelings in different ways and to varying degrees, for example 'irritated' 'depressed' 'delighted' and 'anxious'. He asks the group or person to match the words and phrases into the appropriate columns.

➤ A drugs information worker lists the beginnings of sentences that give factual information about drugs down the left hand side of the whiteboard. Down the right hand side, she lists the ends of the sentences in a jumbled order and invites a volunteer to match the correct beginning and endings together by drawing different coloured joining lines, under the direction of the group.

The way it works

Matching sentences can be done individually, in pairs or small groups or as a bigger group activity with flip charts and a scribe. There are many variations on this idea, some of which are given here as examples, and some are listed below in 'other things you can do with it.' For those who like to take in information by reading words, searching for the matches can help to reinforce the information contained in the completed sentences.

Tips for using it:

- The aim is to reinforce learning, not failure. Give as much help and encouragement as is needed and keep the activity short and snappy.

- If someone in the group has problems with reading, they may end up more confused about the information because it has been jumbled up. These activities are for those who are quite competent with words, or who have help from someone who is competent with words.

Other things you can do with it

- Words can be matched to pictures instead of other words. For example the name of an emotion can be matched to the picture of a facial expression, or an emoticon.

- This can be a moving around activity, where one person has one half of the match and has to find the person with the other half.

- The second halves of the sentences to be matched can be written on sticky notes so they can be easily stuck next to their matching half on a board.

Writing letters

Letter-writing can be used to explore and express feelings about a person, a dilemma or a situation. These letters need not be sent to anyone. Letter-writing can also be a way of requesting information, making a complaint or campaining. Letters can keep people in touch with someone who doesn't use email or text, such as an elderly relative, or someone in prison or hospital.

Examples

> A young woman who wants to see more of her divorced father writes a 'not to be sent' letter to her mother. This helps her to sort out her thoughts and decide what she wants to say to her mother and how she wants to say it.

> Participants of a small support group write problem page letters based on situations they have experienced, or that someone close to them have experienced. They swap their problem with another group member and each creates a reply for their partner.

> A young woman who has recently argued with her sister writes a letter to herself as if she was her sister, trying to imagine how her sister would view the situation, how she would be feeling and what she might want to say. The young woman talks this through with a counsellor. She then writes a letter to her sister describing how she has felt since the argument and gives it to her sister.

> A group who are campaigning for a skateboard park in the area compose a letter to the council stating their views and asking for further information about plans for the site in question.

The way it works

Letters can be long or short, chatty or formal. A letter is different from an email in that it is less immediate and lends itself to situations where views need to be considered and feelings cooled down before engaging in real life dialogue about an issue. Letters need not be written – they can be dictated, or spoken onto tape if preferred.

8

Tips for using it:

- Clarify the purpose of the letter with the young person.

- Clarify whether they intend to send it, keep it, burn it, throw it away, give it to you or whatever.

- A no-holds-barred letter to someone can contain strong feelings. Be sure the young person understands that an unsent letter won't harm or affect the other person.

- When a letter is actually being sent to someone else, check whether the young person wants any technical assistance.

Other things you can do with it

- Invite young people to form a panel of experts to discuss problem-page letters. Panel members may be instructed to voice opposing viewpoints. The rest of the group is asked to vote on the best solution put forward. However, this may lighten the approach to the issue and is best used when the problems put forward are from magazines rather than an individual's own current dilemmas.

- Follow up goal-setting work by asking the young person to write their goals and action plans in a letter to themselves. Take the letters and post them to the young person at a pre-arranged time, for example two weeks later so they can check the progress they have made by then and be reminded of the steps they were going to take.

Scenario cards

Scenario cards are a useful way of presenting young people with credible characters in situations relevant to the topic under consideration, so they can explore the implications of options open to these characters in this situation.

Examples

→ A *peer mediation skills training group uses scenario cards to examine the skills involved in dealing with situations that may arise.*

→ A *worker introduces a set of scenario cards to his group to generate discussion on the subject of peer pressure.*

→ A *group working on assertiveness training uses scenario cards to practise alternative behaviours.*

The way it works

Each scenario card in a set describes one or more characters in roles and situations relevant to the needs of the group. For example, a scenario card for peer mediation training might say:

You have been asked to mediate between Jenni (13) and Paula (13). They have been close friends since they came to the school, but Jenni recently started going around with a different group and calling Paula names. Paula became very upset and started a fight with Jenni. The teacher who stopped the fight suggested they try a peer mediation session. During the session Jenni says she doesn't want to be Paula's friend any more and Paula, who is usually quite tough, starts to cry. How do you feel when Paula cries? What do you do?

A card like this could be used as the basis for small group discussion, to generate a range of possible responses to the dilemma. If different groups discuss the same dilemma, their responses can be compared.

9

Scenario cards for assertiveness training may describe assertive, passive or aggressive behaviours and ask the group to identify what characterises the three different behaviours (see also **Forum Theatre** and **Role Play or Practice Exercises** in the section on drama).

see page 110 and 120
MORE IDEAS

Tips for using it:

- Scenario cards work well with pairs or groups of up to four people.

- Encourage young people to create their own scenarios for the cards so they reflect young people's experience.

- Give the characters described on the cards names and some personal details, such as 'Crystal is sixteen and is usually the leader in her group'.

- Try not to use situations that closely match the real experience of someone who is working from the card.

- Where possible, ask questions that address the reader's or the character's feelings as well as their actions.

Other things you can do with it

see page 106
MORE IDEAS

- Create a board game using scenario cards with questions on. Give each question multiple choice answers, with a score for each answer on the back of the card. The score indicates the number of moves the player can make around the board (see **Board Games** in the section on moving, sorting and handling).

- You can create hypothetical scenarios when you work with individual young people as well as groups. You could use prepared cards, or just make up scenarios on the spot to match the topic under discussion. Ask the young person what he or she would do in that situation.

Poems and lyrics

Song and rap lyrics are a familiar part of young people's culture. Talking to young people about their favourite artists and encouraging them to write their own poems and lyrics can be a way of engaging about subjects that are important to them. Poems and lyrics can help young people use language, rhyme, rhythm and sometimes humour to express their feelings and get an immediate audience rapport.

Examples

→ A mental health support group creates 'found' poems by cutting up a selection of poems and lyrics and pasting them together to make new poems that link random clippings with their own words and phrases and use repetition for emphasis.

→ A young woman in a pupil referral unit is preparing a project about homelessness. She writes the word 'homeless' in single letters down the left hand side of a sheet of paper then writes a word or sentence that begins with each letter, so the whole forms a 'poem' on this topic.

→ A youth counsellor has a magnetic poetry kit on the side of a filing cabinet in his room. Sometimes young people rearrange the words into lines of poetry that express how they are feeling and this is a good starting point for talking about feelings.

The way it works

Ask young people to bring in the lyrics to their favourite songs and talk about why they like them. Read them aloud together and talk about how they use rhythm, specific images and repetition. Ask them to write about a particular issue or personal experience in the same style.

Poetic writing helps develop a vocabulary of the senses. Bring in some objects, photographs or music and ask questions such as:

- What does it smell like?
- What does the sound remind you of?
- Does it leave a taste in your mouth?
- If you held it or stroked it with your eyes shut, what would it remind you of?
- If you had never been to this place before, how would you feel when you saw it?
- What shapes and colours can you see?
- Who does this person remind you of?
- What comes to mind when you listen to this music?

Invite a performance poet or rap artist to perform and talk about their work.

Tips for using it:

- *Pop stars can be important role models. Encourage young people to talk to you about why they like certain artists, but don't make judgments on the basis of your own values.*

- *Encourage young people to bring in their favourite music and play it in sessions.*

- *Encourage performance from those who are willing. Watch out for those on the sidelines who may join in with a bit of encouragement. Use the audience as 'chorus' if appropriate.*

- *Encourage young people to find their talent then help them find other outlets and opportunities for development.*

Other things you can do with it

- Write up lines from song lyrics as 'Thought for the Day' pocket-sized cards to carry around (see **Reminder Cards** from the section on visuals).

see page 72
MORE IDEAS

- Create a poetry wall using strips of newsprint. Encourage people to post up random lines and verses of their own as well as from their favourite artists.

- Use karaoke backing tracks for young people to write new lyrics to famous songs. Rap or sing them for an audience.

- Compose a group rap, with members of the group taking a few lines each, accompanied by a preset rhythm on a keyboard.

Journals and logs

Many teenagers enjoy keeping diaries, journals and personal logs. At a time when they are experimenting with different ways of being, it can help them to identify feelings, people and things that are important to them. Journals provide material to reflect on later and explore patterns of behaviour and reasons for choices.

Examples

➡ A disorganised young woman starts to keep a time management log to she work out how much time her regular activities actually take. This will eventually help her to plan her activities more realistically.

➡ A young man who has recently moved to the UK starts to write 'The story of my life'. This is a collection of important moments, friends, family and developments. He uses drawings, photos, newspaper articles, stories and recollections to fill the pages of his diary. He shares it with his Connexions worker.

➡ A young woman who self-harms starts to keep a journal. This contains some very personal writings about important moments and feelings during the day. She finds this helpful in tracing the patterns that lead to her self-harming behaviour. Her psychiatric nurse suggests that she writes about positive experiences too, and any patterns she notices in connection with these.

The way it works

Journals and logs take many forms. You can prepare specially formatted pages, such as timed sections for daily logs, or the young person might prefer to develop their own style of journal.

Many of the other suggestions in this handbook lend themselves to inclusion in a journal, such as letters, poems, photographs and drawings.

If a young person is daunted by the idea of starting a journal, you could gather samples of personal material that has already been created in your work together, put them in a folder and suggest that this is the start of a journal.

The young person might want to share their journal with you on a regular basis, or just talk with you about things that have arisen from keeping the journal.

Daily logs can be used to find patterns and opportunities for change.

Tips for using it

- Encourage the young person to decorate the cover of the journal and take pride in its presentation.

- Be clear from the outset how the journal is to be used and who will see it.

- Offer to keep the journal in a safe place and let the young person add to it regularly, if they don't have a safe place of their own to keep it.

- Avoid focusing solely on a negative theme. Journals can be useful for picking out patterns around self-harm or eating disorders, but this shouldn't be their sole focus. Show that you value the whole of the person, not just their 'problem.'

- A journal doesn't have to follow a realistic chronology. Past, present and future, fact, fantasy and dreams can all find a place in a personal journal.

Other things you can do with it

- In groupwork, encourage the group to keep an ongoing log of their work together. This may be a collection of session evaluation sheets, or a diary of the process of a group activity.

- In individual work, you and the young person could write a brief summary of each session you have together. These could go into a journal that you can review from time to time to assess progress.

- As a worker it's useful to keep your own professional reflective journal. It can help you to pick out your own strengths and weaknesses, express your feelings, or notice patterns of behaviour

Communicating through visuals

Communicating through visuals isn't about being 'artistic' or able to draw and paint. Some young people have an extraordinary ability to draw, paint, sculpt or create cartoon characters and their talents should be celebrated, but visuals can also be used by those who are less confident in creating visual art. As in communicating through the written word, creativity, feelings and thoughts can be expressed through manipulating 'found' images, through stick drawings and critical viewing, and via the use of new technologies. These activities can be a welcome relief to young people who feel uncomfortable expressing themselves in written words. Again, you need to be aware of any special needs of the young people you are working with, such as visual or mobility impairments and how they would prefer to deal with these needs with regard to activities that focus on communicating through visuals.

Contents

Comic strips

Comic strip stories and characters are a familiar form to many young people and can be used to convey information, describe dilemmas and explore situations, relationships and decisions in an accessible way.

Examples

➤ A group of young people is campaigning on an environmental issue. They create a comic strip character who appears on all campaign publicity alongside the message the group wants to convey. They give the character a catchy, memorable name.

➤ A young deaf man creates a comic strip story that details the experiences of a deaf young man at a party with hearing people. The speech bubbles are blanked out except for the thoughts of the central character.

➤ In a training group for peer educators in sex and relationships education, two girls use pictures from magazines and newspapers to create a photostory that details the lack of communication between a girl and boy who are about to have sex for the first time. They show the photostory to the rest of the training group, who discuss what captions should go with each frame of the story.

The way it works

Consider using a comic strip story to convey information to young people, for instance to advertise your group and the issues you deal with. Narrative information is often easy to remember and comic strip characters are a familiar feature to many young people. Involve young people in producing this work. You can also use the comic strip form to look at current dilemmas young people are facing. Use pre-formatted sheets with four blank frames. Start with the last frame. Whatever scene is in this frame is the cliffhanger – the dilemma the young person you are working with faces at the moment. Who is involved in this dilemma? What do we see in the frame? Who is saying or thinking what? Ask the young person to fill in this frame and then work backwards. The previous three frames show how this situation arose. Who was involved? How can this be summed up in three clearly distinct scenes? Ask the young person to draw these.

What would they like to see happen in the next strip of four frames? What would be in the last frame? Is this likely to happen? Is this in the young person's control, at least partly? What would they need to do to make it happen? Approaching personal dilemmas in this way is a very visual and memorable way of considering alternative actions (see also **Encouraging and Motivating for Change** in the section on communicating for different purposes).

see page 26 MORE IDEAS

Tips for using it:

- Always give the characters names. If the dilemma is a personal one, depersonalise it by giving the characters different names

- Young people don't need to be artists to create personal cartoon strips. These can be done with stick people, like a storyboard.

Other things you can do with it

- Use a photo as the start of a story – as the first frame. Then draw the remaining frames as a cartoon.

- Use computer animation packages to create cartoon stories on the computer.

- Cut up the separate frames of a photostrip story and stick them onto different cards. Ask young people to arrange them in any order and describe what's going on.

- Create comic strip stories with alternative endings. What are the repercussions of each ending?

- These alternative endings can also be explored through **Forum Theatre** in the section on drama.

see page 110 MORE IDEAS

Photographs

Professional photographs often evoke an emotional response and can be used to help young people develop emotional literacy. Personal photo albums can help a young person make sense of their own life story.

Young people can express their view of the world by taking photos, or they can use them to become familiar with a new situation, new surroundings, new staff or a new journey.

Examples

 A girl who is dealing with the death of a grandfather collects images of the neighbourhood over the last fifty years. This corresponds to the time her grandfather lived there. She adds her own thoughts and stories to the photos based on what she remembers her grandfather saying.

 A young men's group collects and discusses images of young men in the media. They explore questions about how young men are represented in print, on TV and in film and why.

 As part of a project on bullying, group members go round the school taking photographs of places where bullying often takes place. They create a display of these photos, along with a suggestion box for comments on how these areas could be made safer.

 As part of a consultation with young people with communication difficulties about a service they use, photos of the staff and facilities are used to prompt responses in face-to-face interviews.

The way it works

Photographs can be used in many different ways, some of which are shown in the examples.

Collect interesting photographs. Simply spreading them out and asking young people to choose a photograph that appeals to them can be a good starting point for discussion. What was it that appealed to them? Does anyone in the photo remind them of anyone they know? How do they think the people in the photo are feeling? How do they know? (This can lead into discussion of body language and the way people communicate without words – see also **Non-verbal Language** in the section on drama.)

see page 132
MORE IDEAS

If you are working with a group on their transition from primary to secondary school, it can be helpful for them to have photos of staff and classrooms that they have visited on a preliminary visit and are likely to encounter again.

Tips for using it:

- *If you are making your own collection of photos from newspapers and magazines, they will last longer if you stick them onto card and laminate them.*

- *Some publishers sell specially created sets of photos on specific themes for educational purposes.*

Other things you can do with it

Use photos in creating posters on a theme (see **Posters** in this section). Create a photo gallery of pictures of the group when they were younger than they are now, (check that everyone has access to photos from their past, and that they are willing to show them).

see page 64
MORE IDEAS

Charts and scales

Charts and scales help young people to see patterns and processes more clearly, and express the intensity of their experiences even when they are uncomfortable with words, or with talking about their feelings.

Examples

 A counsellor is working with a boy who has low self-esteem. She asks the boy to draw a self-esteem chart, with numbers from 0-10 down the side, and different aspects of his life and personality along the bottom. Aspects of his life are: school, football, looks, family, relationships. He rates his self-esteem in each of these areas. It is lower than 5 in all areas except sport. He feels reassured that there is one area where he feels good about himself.

 In anger management training, a girl draws a thermometer. On the same page, she lists six things that make it rise, with the one that winds her up the most at the top, and small irritations at the bottom. She uses this as the basis for recognising what makes her flare up and how quickly it can happen. Then she looks at alternative ways of responding to her angry feelings.

The way it works

You can use ready made templates (for example, make a photocopiable image of a thermometer) or you can ask the young person to draw their own. It is often more meaningful to the user if it's their own creation, but if you are working in a group, templates might be easier. Use the young person's completed charts or scales as a starting point for discussion:

- Does the young person notice any pattern emerging?

- Does anything surprise them?

- Can they think of ways of responding differently to just one of their anger triggers?

Representing inner processes visually makes them harder to ignore when they happen again.

Tips for using it:

- Find some books that use statistics. You will see a great variety of ways of presenting charts and scales. Be imaginative.

- Charts and scales are particularly helpful if a young person is keeping a log or journal. They can look for patterns over time and may understand more clearly what affects them and consider how to gain power over their responses.

- A young person who finds it hard to discuss their feelings may find it easier to answer a 'scale of 1-10' question about their emotions.

Other things you can do with it

- Scaling can also be used spontaneously, in discussion with a young person. For example, 'So how would you rate the way you feel about that today, on a scale of 1-10, if ten is fantastic and one is completely gutted?' is an intervention that could be appropriate during a conversation about an issue the young person has discussed with you before.

- Charts can be used to show the results of opinion polls on a particular topic.

- Instead of preset marks on a thermometer or scale, you could use a picture of a cup or glass and ask the young person to mark 'how full' the cup is today (for example full of worries or hopes).

Posters

These may be educational, campaigning or inspiring. They can combine words and images and provide a powerful and succinct way of conveying a message about a topic. Getting a message across via a poster expresses the value of this message for the people who create the poster.

see page 40
MORE IDEAS

Examples

➔ A group of teenage mums draws up a poster of their young mums' charter (see **Charters and Bills of Rights** in the section on the written word).

➔ A quit smoking group makes a poster of 'Scary facts about smoking.'

➔ A young man about to leave foster care and move into supported housing creates a poster for a movie called 'My Life'. He has included a picture of the star who will play the leading role and has decided that this is a rags to riches story which will end successfully. His key worker follows this line of thought and talks with him about the steps this character might take to overcome obstacles in the plot.

➔ A group addressing exam stress creates a poster called '10 golden rules for sailing through exams.'

The way it works

Presenting information or ideas on a topic via a poster means a young person begins by identifying the most important or essential messages. The next step is to decide how to convey them simply through words and pictures that are eye-catching and memorable. A poster may be needed for a campaign, in which case copies must be made, or the poster may be for personal use, as inspiration or as a reminder of useful information. Posters can be created by individuals or in small groups.

Make available plenty of materials, such as paper, photos, magazines, scissors, glue, paints, coloured pens. Professional looking posters can also be created with the aid of computer software. Photos and images can be manipulated to achieve different effects.

Tips for using it

- Make sure the young people know exactly what it is they want to convey and who they want to convey it to.

- What response do they want to get from the people who see the poster? Is their poster likely to achieve this response?

- Encourage them to sketch out more than one version and try them out on people first. Do others immediately understand what the poster is saying?

- Introduce different types of posters and discuss whether they work and how.

- If posters are created by young people as part of a group activity on a theme, consider whether there is a public place to display these posters, with the group's consent.

Other things you can do with it

Posters can be reduced in size to become leaflets, handed out to people to interest them in the topic, campaign or event. This gives scope for more detailed information to be given on the reverse side.

Drawing relationships

Drawing relationships is a way for young people to explore feelings and perceptions about the way they relate to friends and family. They don't need to be able to draw well as these activities work just as well with 'stick people' as more detailed drawings.

Examples

 A boy is having some difficulty making friends and keeping them. As he is very quiet and finds it hard to talk about his problems, his head of year at school suggests that he draws a little sketch showing himself with other classmates. She tells him the drawing doesn't have to be realistic, but she should be able to tell by looking at it how close the boy feels to his classmates. She hopes that this will provide a way in to discussing and managing the problem from the boy's perspective.

 As part of their family therapy 'homework' the members of a family containing two teenagers are asked to draw a diagram of how closely the adults and children related to each other ten years ago, and a diagram of how closely they relate now. In the following session, they will compare their diagrams and discuss any changes in terms of what happens when families grow up.

The way it works

If you are working with a young person on their relationships with others, you could ask them to draw a quick sketch of themselves in relation to someone they have talked about, who is or has been significant in their lives. If they need prompts, you could ask:

- Do you feel bigger or smaller or equal to them?
- Do you feel close or is there a distance between you?
- Are you hugging or fighting? Smiling or crying? Relaxed or tense?

Ask questions about the drawing, but don't make assumptions. If it feels helpful, you could ask the young person to draw the same relationship from the other person's point of view. Do they imagine that the other person sees it the same way?
Is this the way the young person often feels in relationships?
The same activity can be used to explore the way a young person feels in groups. Are they in front or behind? Alone or included? Upright or trampled on? Carrying others or being supported?

Tips for using it:

- *Don't end the session on a negative note. If the picture shows that the young person doesn't feel good in a relationship, help them to think of something they can do to feel better in this or a future relationship. Ask them to draw this new version too.*

Other things you can do with it

- Collect photographs of people in groups and pairs, showing different relationships between them. Instead of asking the young person to draw their own relationship, you could ask them to identify the photograph that is most like how they feel in this relationship, or in a group.

- Ask the young person to choose an animal to represent themselves in a relationship. What animal is the other person? Ask them to draw how these animals are together. What animal would the young person ideally like to be? How would the picture look then? Bear in mind that some cultural groups are not comfortable with animals representing humans, so check with the young person if this approach is OK and find alternatives if necessary.

Metaphors

A visual metaphor is when a concrete image of one thing implies an abstract idea about something else. For example a heart signifies love and a lion signifies courage. Young people can express themselves in a metaphorical drawing, such as 'I'm taking a leap in the dark' and picture positive outcomes – 'a safe landing.' Or they can use prepared images with common associations to explore a topic.

Examples

→ A careers group uses worksheets on which there are drawings of a crossroads, with different paths to choose from. They are asked to name the paths and think about which one they might choose to follow if they had to choose right now.

→ A young man who has had some difficult experiences recently is invited to draw the landscape of the last six months, using landscape imagery such as hills, forests, tropical islands, mountains and bridges to represent the journey he has been on. It helps him to see himself as having survived a great deal and arrived intact.

→ A group of school leavers are working on the ending of their time at school together. They are presented with a cardboard box. This represents a time capsule, containing mementos of their school days. These mementos will be drawings of significant items, memories and things that sum up the present moment, rather than the things themselves. The group is asked to do their drawings and put them in the box. They are reminded that they can revisit this moment in time as often as they choose, in their memories.

The way it works

You can prepare some template outlines as worksheets, ready for a young person to fill in with their own words and images, (such as 'My window on the world' divided into four frames) or encourage the young person to draw the metaphor in their own way. You can get ideas just by listening to the metaphors the young people use in their everyday speech. Some drawings can become whole group activities, such as the 'hall of fame' where biographical details and photos or drawings of group members can be pinned up so that group members can get to know each other.

Tips for using it

- Drawings can provide an alternative to words as a way of expressing feelings or examining experiences. It may not be necessary to talk about it as well. Follow the young person's lead on this.

- Don't be tempted to analyse or interpret a young person's drawings. Symbols and colours may have different meanings for different people or in different cultures.

- Some young people find drawings a very powerful way of expressing themselves. Be careful of using very powerful visual imagery (for instance concerning death or depression) without proper support and training.

- Always ask the young person what they want to do with the drawings they have worked on.

Other things you can do with it

- Use different materials to create an island on which the group or individual lives. They can create all the things they want to have on the island, and for the time being, the things they don't want can be put to sea in boats.

- Ask the group to create a snakes and ladders board game. What is on the squares that take you up the ladders? What is on the squares that lead you down the snakes? (See **Board Games** in the section on moving, sorting and handling).

see page 106
MORE IDEAS

Collage and montage

Collage and montage work in similar ways. Both use a variety of images to make one whole picture. For collage, the emphasis is on the selection of different materials and textures, words and pictures, to represent a theme, and in montage the emphasis is more on building up an image through repetition and manipulation of smaller elements.

Examples

→ Young people in a healthy eating group each draw an image of healthy food. Then they cut up these images and use them, along with magazine photos and articles and food labels, to create a bigger image that gives an overall and immediate message about eating healthily.

→ A young woman working on self esteem chooses a favourite photograph of herself and 'writes' her name large in repeated copies of this photo.

The way it works

These activities can be used to reinforce positive messages learnt from discussion and other work, or to explore an issue non-verbally. The more materials you have available, the more a young person can use tactile senses as well as visual to communicate what they want to. You will need big backing sheets such as flip chart sheets, newsprint or wallpaper for collage and montage to be mounted on.

Tips for using it

- Collect lots of different fabrics, magazines, card, paper, string, glue, paints, crayons, chalks, scissors and pens for this work. You may need to have separate boxes to keep different types of materials in, and store the leftovers neatly at the end of a session.

- You could use ready-made outlines for montage, such as a house, the planet earth, a hot air balloon. The images used to fill in the outline would relate to the concept of the original outline.

- Young people can work in pairs to prepare collages or montages. Different pairs might work on different aspects of the same issue.

- Consider how and where the finished products can be displayed.

Other things you can do with it

You can use computers for creating and printing montage. The way photos and images can be manipulated on screen, and copied into other images lends itself to this sort of activity.

Reminder cards

Reminder cards are the size of business cards and can easily fit in a young person's pocket, wallet or purse. They can be used for personal reminders, for inspirational quotations and for details to be shown or given to other people.

Examples

 A young person prints C210 on a small card and keeps it in their pocket where they can feel it and hold it. C210 is a reminder for them to 'Count to Ten' before responding if someone is winding them up.

 A young person out of prison and on tag keeps a 'countdown' card in their pocket. This shows one mark for every day they are on tag. The young person ticks off the days as a visual reminder to motivate themselves to avoid trouble.

 A youth worker creates cards that each show inspirational messages chosen by young people. She gives them out to her group as 'thoughts for the day.'

The way it works

You can buy or cut up a set of blank business cards. The cards should be designed and made by or in consultation with the young person they are for. Help them take pride in the way the cards look, so they feel more ownership of them and therefore of the reminder messages on them. The cards should be made after you have worked with the young people on a particular issue. Touching and handling the card is often enough of a reminder about what the card says.

Tips for using it:

- Laminate the cards or buy plastic card holders to keep the cards in.

- You can buy sheets of card and encourage the young person to make up their cards on computer, using software for making business cards. Print them out onto card.

Other things you can do with it

- Use this idea in conjunction with **Charters and Bills** in the section on Communicating through the written word. A young person can have each one of the rights on a list written up separately on cards to remind themselves that, for example, 'I have the right to sit in class without being bullied'.

see page 40 MORE IDEAS

- At the end of a session, split the group into threes and ask each person to write something they have appreciated about the other two people, on a card. Everyone then has two compliment cards to take away and keep.

- A young person could make an agreement with teachers that they can leave the classroom for short periods if they are likely to have an outburst, or if they are feeling very upset. The code for this request can be written on a card, so the young person only has to show the card to be given permission to leave.

Gingerbread shapes

The gingerbread outline is a shape most people can manage to draw, even if they don't consider themselves artistic. Because it has a large outline it lends itself to exploring two aspects of a topic. One aspect can be drawn or written about inside the shape, and the other outside. For example, this could illustrate what someone feels like, alongside how they may look to others.

Examples

 A *drugs awareness session uses a gingerbread activity. In groups of four, young people are given a flip chart sheet with the instruction to draw a large gingerbread shape on it. On the inside of the shape they draw or write all the ways in which a young person might keep themselves healthy and how this would benefit them. On the outside they draw or write all the pressures a young person might feel to engage in unhealthy activities, even though they know the associated health risks. When the groups are ready, they compare their results and discuss the implications of what they have described.*

 A *young men's group uses a gingerbread activity to look at the contrast between how they think they should appear (the outside of the gingerbread) and how they sometimes feel (the inside). This leads to discussion and other activities aiming to explore whether and why men keep their feelings hidden.*

The way it works

Gingerbread shape activities are effective on a large piece of paper, such as a flip chart sheet, even when you are only working with one person. The outline should take up a big part of the sheet, but leave some surrounding room. The inside perspective will often contain a more private reality. Encourage young people to use images as well as words in their representation of different ideas.

Tips for using it

- Use a thick pen for the outlines and have plenty of coloured pens available. Encourage the group to all get involved. This activity doesn't need a group 'scribe'.

- Don't have more than four people in each group, or they will find it hard to all access the shape at the same time.

- If there is someone in your group who would find it hard to get down on the floor, make sure groups can work at tables for this.

Other things you can do with it

- You can use these shapes in place of **Quick Thoughts** at the start of a topic, but make sure that they have the same quality of including uncensored ideas from everybody.

see page 42 MORE IDEAS

Watching television

Watching television is part of many people's daily life and conversation. Young people often compare their own situations with those of characters in films or TV programmes. These references can be used to help the young person explore the issue in question. Watching television can also be a deliberate activity with young people, using specially chosen dramas or educational programmes to illustrate specific points.

Examples

 A girl visiting a school counsellor continually compares herself to a character in a well known drama series based in a prison. The counsellor knows this series and is able to discuss it on the girl's terms. She understands that the girl is really expressing something about feeling trapped and under pressure, but it is more important that the girl can express this, than that the counsellor knows all the factual details at this point. She knows that the girl has been under pressure within her family since her mother left home. When the girl mentions the character again, the counsellor asks what the girl imagines will happen to her, but at no point does she ask the girl whether she identifies with this character.

 A group working on sex and relationships watch a drama created specially for use in sex and relationships education and complete the tasks suggested in the accompanying notes.

The way it works

Try to be familiar with the television programmes watched by the young people you work with. Be ready to talk about life as lived by a well known soap character, as it may create an opportunity to talk about real life dilemmas, or to find out why a young person identifies strongly with a particular character. This applies to pop stars and reality TV characters as well as TV drama.

Many organisations now create videos on topics of interest concerning young people. Unless you know and trust the organisation, it can be hard to know whether the video is likely to be useful, but you should be able to inspect a copy before buying, or have a period in which you can send it back for a full refund. Most videos are now accompanied by teaching notes, though you may prefer to create your own activities in relation to the video. When you are watching a video on a certain subject, try to watch it interactively. That is, make sure the young people have questions that they want answered, or that they are looking out for certain things.

Tips for using it

- Use short extracts or break them up with questions and activities.

- Make sure everyone can see the screen and hear the sound. Some videos have subtitling for people with hearing difficulties.

- Watch young people's reactions as they watch the extracts. What engages them or turns them off?

Other things you can do with it

As well as watching television, young people can plan and make their own video films (see **Making Videos** in the section on moving, handling and sorting).

see page 126
MORE IDEAS

You can pause a television programme to ask questions like: 'What do you think this character is feeling now? What do you think she should do next? What would you do if it were you?' (For more on this freeze frame approach, see **Freeze the Scene** in the section on drama.)

see page 112
MORE IDEAS

Drawing signatures

During their teenage years, people often experiment with different versions of who they are, whilst working on a grown up identity that suits them. As part of this process, they often create new signatures. They may also have new official things to sign as part of becoming an adult. Developing art work from signatures can provide a good focus for discussion about identity and individuality.

Examples

On a creative arts residential weekend, a group of young people draw their signatures on a large sheet of paper on the wall. Around the signatures, they draw or write things that connect with their names: nicknames, pet names and other associations such as famous people who share one of their names. They draw and write in colours they associate with their names. Near their names, they create a tag, like graffitti artists, using non-toxic spray paints. During the activity, the facilitator encourages discussion about what their names mean to them (see also **Graffitti Wall** in this section).

see page 82
MORE IDEAS

The way it works

You can use signatures as an art activity with individuals and groups. With individuals, you may be able to go into greater depth about positive and negative associations with the young person's name. For example there may be a sense of loss over other family members, or the young person's name may have been changed on adoption or on moving to this country. Or a name may have been the focus of bullying. Encourage a sense of pride in the creation of this piece of name art even if there are some negative feelings involved. In group work, encourage respect for each other's names and their visual representations. You may not be able to address negative connotations in the same way in a large group, but make sure you acknowledge the complexity of feelings people have about their names. Tags can be a good way of making a fresh start with names.

Tips for using it:

- This isn't a good 'opener' for a new group, as there are too many personal issues connected with names, and you need to build mutual respect in the group first.

- Bring in examples of famous people's signatures, autographs, and pictures of tags.

- This can stimulate discussion about tagging, art and vandalism. Why do people do it? Is it art?

Other things you can do with it

- Young people could start by drawing round the shape of their hand, and then do the signature inside this. The shape of their hand will be unique as well as their signature.

- Young people could develop their own personal icon to go with their signature. There are many examples of 'avatars' on the Internet. An avatar is a picture that you choose to represent yourself, for example in an Internet chat room, a personal web page or weblog. It originates from a Sanskrit word to do with the incarnation of a deity. This could lead to discussions about Internet identities, safety on the net, and alternative identities.

- Issues around proof of identity are prominent for this age group, who are often challenged over their age and identity.

Mapping networks

Mapping out a particular network of people, organisations, roles, tasks and decisions is a useful way of showing how these relate to each other and how each can influence the others. It can help young people to think about 'the bigger picture.' If the map relates to a group task, it can be displayed as a reminder of what is to be done and who is to do it.

Examples

→ A social worker is helping a young woman in foster care to make sense of her family relationships, about which she has strong but contradictory feelings. The social worker helps the young woman to draw a family tree. The young woman also wants to include some of the relationships she has built up with her foster carers' family. After discussion, she finds a new design for the tree that enables her to incorporate her closeness to foster carers without losing her connection with her own family. Creating the tree also helps her to identify gaps in her knowledge about her family and she discusses these with her social worker.

→ A young man who is trying to cut down his drinking draws a map of the people and situations that influence his drinking, positively and negatively. He extends this map to include resources such as websites and other activities. It helps him to see the whole picture of the influences on his drinking and the support systems that are available to him.

The way it works

Young people often feel empowered by seeing the bigger picture and understanding how they can influence and be influenced by others. You can use creative ways of illustrating these networks, from spidergraphs to blossoming trees with individual stick-on leaves. At the start of a group task, a mapping activity might be the next step after a quick thoughts session. For instance, decisions can be made at this stage about who is performing what role in the group, and what their tasks are. Deciding this at the beginning and displaying it will save confusion or neglect later. Network maps can also be used to show where a young person can find support on a particular issue. The stages of turning a goal into action can be mapped out, showing the different people who may be involved or affected by the decision at any stage.

Tips for using it

- Let the ideas and the form of the map come from the young person themselves. Ask questions when they have finished, to check that they have included everything necessary.

- You can use sticky notes to put different elements of the map onto the page and rearrange them. When the arrangement is finalised, the sticky notes can be replaced by a permanent drawing.

- Use different coloured lines to represent different relationships between separate elements on the map.

Other things you can do with it

see page 118 and 120 MORE IDEAS

- You can do mapping as a 'live' activity using group members (see **Sculpting** and **Role Play or Practice Exercises** in the drama section).

- You can use network-mapping to talk about boundaries. Use a template of concentric circles. Ask the young person to write their name in the middle circle. Label the other circles with different levels of relationship, such as 'people I know well and trust', 'people I talk to but don't know well' and so on. Ask the young person to write the names of relevant people in each circle. You can use this as a springboard for discussing how people know who to trust and what behaviours are appropriate with different people.

Graffitti wall

The graffitti wall is a great way of encouraging young people to express whatever they want to express about a topic. It may be used at the end of a session or workshop for evaluation, or just as a way of creating a highly visual group expression on a topic.

Examples

 At the end of a training session for peer mediators, trainees are invited to comment on what they liked and didn't like by spraying their comments on the 'wall' with non-toxic spray paints.

 At the start of work with a group who have not worked together before, digital photos are taken of each group member. These photos are printed out and pinned onto a strip of paper on the wall. Next to their own photo, group members spray or draw their signature or tag and the name they want to be known by.

 As part of an environmental project, a group displays a poster they have made, and sets up a 'graffitti wall' next to it, for classmates to comment on 'The world in ten years' time.'

The way it works

Use long rolls of newsprint, or brick-patterned wallpaper and pin it up along a wall. You can get non-toxic spray paints in different colours. Use this activity to generate free expression on the topic. It can help the more timid group members to express themselves too. Short poems and drawings can be sprayed as well as single words and phrases. Give a clear time for the activity so people work quickly. Once some comments go up, it gives others ideas too. Make sure there's plenty of space for everyone and encourage those who are not so assertive to take up as much room as they need.

13

Tips for using it

- It's a great activity to do to music.

- Use non-toxic paints.

- Use this activity as an opportunity to talk about graffitti, vanadalism and responsibility for the environment, and rights versus responsibilities.

- You may need to agree on some rules about not being personally offensive, or refer back to the group contract.

- Arrange protective clothing and protection for surroundings. Leave time for the group to clear up after themselves.

- You can create a similar airbrush effect by using 'blow pens' and marker pens with thick tips – and it's not as messy.

Other things you can do with it

- Some youth projects have negotiated with the local council to have specific public walls designated for the use of young people to demonstrate their street art. Encourage young people to take a pride in these walls.

- Create a mural using other materials as well as spray paint.

Communicating through moving, handling and sorting

Activities that involve moving around can be good energisers at the start of a session or in the middle, when energy or attention are flagging. People have very different thresholds in relation to their ability to sit still, and many young people will respond well to activities that allow for the opportunity to move around. For some young people, information goes in better and learning is more complete when they have a physical involvement with the subject matter, either by handling items that relate to it, or moving around whilst taking it in. Moving sorting and handling activities can easily combine with drama, written word activities and visuals. Try to be aware of difficulties people might have with mobility or handling. These difficulties are not always obvious and young people don't necessarily want to have attention drawn to themselves. Nonetheless, you should try to cater for levels of pain and fatigue some young people might experience.

Contents

Four corners

Four corners involves designating each corner of the room with different properties and moving the group around to explore the four properties. It can be used as a quick energiser in the middle of a session or at the start of a session as a way of generating ideas on a topic.

Examples

see page 44
MORE IDEAS

 During a session on drugs education, the worker labels the four corners of the room with the name of four different illegal substances used by young people. In the middle of a session, especially if energy is flagging, divide the group into four and send one group to each corner, giving them three minutes to come back with a list of all the things they know about this substance. Display the lists. Move the groups around so they read each others' lists and add to the information given, or mark up queries. Leave a few minutes for questions and comments (see also **Ideas Exhibition** in the section on the written word).

During a session on any topic, a worker occasionally splits the group into four and sends each group to a different corner of the room. The corners are designated as different animals, for example 'lion, rabbit, frog, giraffe.' The groups are given three minutes to come up with all the associations they can make between the topic under discussion and their animal. This works well as an energiser in mid-session.

 In the middle of a session on self-esteem, the worker divides the group into four and sends each group to one corner. He tells the groups that their corner has just been visited by someone from another planet where everyone has high self-esteem. Groups are given five minutes to appoint one member as the extra-terrestrial visitor and interview them about how life on their planet makes high self-esteem a possibility for everyone. A spokesperson for the group feeds back with the results of the interview.

The way it works

Use it when energy is sagging. Have a set of ideas such as this handy and spring them on the group when they are least expecting to have to go off to a different part of the room and talk to other people and come up with something collectively in a hurry. The more you emphasise the time pressure, the more energy will be raised.

Tips for using it

- Treat this lightly. It may not shine a lot of light on the topic (though you may be surprised) but it will help energise minds and bodies so the rest of the session may be more useful.

- Put some energetic music on at the same time.

Other things you can do with it

- This can also work with individuals. 'If I were to call each of these four corners happy, sad, worried and angry, which one would you be in at the moment?' Allow for the fact that they might not identify with any of the feelings you name.

Symbolic objects

Symbolic objects can be any objects that 'stand in' for someone or something else, or for abstract ideas and feelings. Using symbolic objects can help young people to express and explore situations and issues that are hard to discuss. Seeing, handling and arranging concrete symbolic objects can help young people gain a fresh perspective on a problem and feel empowered to handle it.

Examples

 *A young man is exploring a situation concerning himself in relation to a group. The worker asks if he would like to use stones, buttons or other objects to represent members of that group and himself. The way the young man arranges the stones makes clear how he perceives himself in relation to the group, and how he views others in the group in relation to each other. The young man then rearranges the stones to show how he would prefer to see the situation. He discusses with the worker the steps he could take to make this happen and she helps him to consider the implications and possible responses to these steps (see also **Drawing Relationships** in the section on visuals).*

see page 66
MORE IDEAS

 At the start of a small group session about sex and relationships, a collection of miniature animals is spread on the table in the middle of the group. The worker asks group members to choose an animal they like the look of, and tell their partner what it is that appeals to them about this animal. They may hold on to the animal for the remainder of the session.

The way it works

Any object can be used to symbolise something else. Even a ketchup bottle or a spoon may illustrate someone's point if these are the only objects available. You can help young people to express themselves by joining in their symbolic world. 'So you're saying it's hard to get from here (the spoon) to here (the ketchup bottle) without getting bullied? What do you need to make this journey safer for you?' You can also use symbolic objects in more deliberate ways. 'Do you want to use the buttons to show me who is able to help you make the change you're aiming to make?' The main principles are that the young person is in charge and you should follow their lead, helping them with your observations. Don't move the objects yourself.

Tips for using it

- Don't interpret or analyse. You can make observations about what's going on, such as, 'I notice this stone is quite far away from the others' and wait for the young person to elaborate. But don't leap to conclusions and take the young person with you. And don't pressurise a young person to explain any more than they want to. A piece of work that involves handling and rearranging symbolic objects can be very satisfying for the person doing it, even if there isn't much said, or much explanation of what's happening.

- Talk about the object by giving it its concrete name, for example 'this stone' or 'this lion'. Don't use the name of the person represented even if the young person has said 'This is my mum' or 'This is my best friend.'

- Keep a collection of objects lying around. It's useful to have some natural objects such as pieces of wood, stones and feathers, and some artificially made objects such as miniature animals and mini bean bags. If possible, find objects with different characters so there's lots of choice for representing different people.

Other things you can do with it

As a way of helping a new group to bond, suggest they create a joint symbolic object to represent the group. For example, they could make a small ship out of cardboard and give it a name. This is the ship that will contain the group on its journey together. The joint activity and the process of choosing a name, is an important part of learning to work together. The metaphor of the ship and the journey can be referred to again as work with the group progresses.

Continuum lines

These activities are a way of getting a snapshot of different opinions and characteristics within a group, and encouraging discussion about the relative value of statements about a given topic.

Examples

 As a warm up to work on self-confidence, the group leader reads out a series of statements in turn such as, 'I feel confident walking into a room full of strangers' and 'I am very good at playing my favourite sport.' One end of the room is designated 'I completely agree with this statement', and the other is designated 'I don't agree at all'. As each statement is read out, group members move to a position in the room that represents their level of agreement with the statement. For each statement ask for a comment from someone in the middle of the line and someone at each end, to explain why they have placed themselves there.

 In another group of young people, cards are distributed containing descriptions of potentially dangerous activities young people might be involved in. Group members arrange themselves in order, according to whether they consider the activity on their card to be very dangerous or safe. They stand in line without speaking at first and then discuss the relative danger of their activity with the people on either side of them, rearranging themselves accordingly. When a new line is established, each person reads out what is on their card and everyone in the group joins in the discussion about whether people have placed themselves in the 'right' order along the line.

The way it works

You can use the whole room and the whole group to move around and depict these relative positions. This is a lively energetic way of gaining different opinions on a topic. It also allows for the quieter ones to express an opinion. In individual work, the same activity can be done using stones, or statements on cards that need to be arranged in order. Continuum line activities can raise interesting aspects of an issue. In the example above on dangerous activities, it raises questions such as 'dangerous for whom?' 'Is the danger short term or long term?' It can also prompt discussion about how people assess risk before they act.

Tips for using it:

- With a big group, these activities can become engrossing and take quite a lot of time. The shorter version is the agree/disagree version described in the first example given. Agreeing on an order of relative statements is often complex and time-consuming but worthwhile.

- Prepare your statements carefully. If you are using the agree/disagree format, make sure you have enough variety that no-one will be at the same end of the line throughout. If you are using the relative values format, test out the statements beforehand for yourself or with colleagues.

- In a very big group, you might want to have two continuum lines with the same set of statements and see if they come to the same arrangement. If not, what are the differences?

Other things you can do with it

- The agree/disagree version could be conducted as a questionnaire (See **Quizzes and Questionnaires** in the section on communicating through the written word)

see page 38
MORE IDEAS

- The relative values version can be done with CDs or stones in individual work

Moving circles

This activity is sometimes called a carousel. It provides a way for everyone to get a chance to have their say on an issue while someone else listens. It is useful for making sure the quiet ones have a chance to speak without feeling as if they are under the spotlight in a big group. This is also a way of practising listening to someone else and demonstrating this.

Examples

 A group of young people is doing a project on the impact of the media on young people. They begin by using moving circles to examine a wide range of views that may be held by groups such as young people, parents, teachers, older people, journalists and programme makers.

The way it works

Divide a group of ten or more into two groups. Ask one group to take their chairs and form a circle facing outward. Now ask the remaining group to sit outside the first circle, with each person facing someone in the inner circle, so there are two concentric circles facing each other. Give each pair a pair of cards ('A' and 'B'). The inner circle person takes the 'A' card and the outer one takes 'B.' Each pair of cards has opposing statements about an issue. Whether or not the holder of the 'A' card agrees with the view on their card, they have one minute to argue the case for this viewpoint. Their partner 'B' then has half a minute to feed back to them what they heard, before arguing the opposing case, as detailed on their card. 'A' then feeds back what they have heard for half a minute. Give each pair another minute in which to discuss their own real views on the topic before moving on. At a given signal, both parties leave their cards on their chairs and the 'A's' and 'B's both move round to their right so that everyone has a new partner and a new viewpoint on a different topic. Repeat the process.

Tips for using it

- Be very clear with your instructions. Give them one at a time, allowing each instruction to be followed before you go on to the next. Otherwise people will start moving in all directions.

- Listeners should be told in advance that they will be expected to feed back what their partner says.

- If the discussion is too quiet and polite, invite the group to get more passionate about what they are saying, by exaggerating their views. It can be liberating for timid young people to have permission to be very opinionated.

- This activity really does need an even number in the group. If you don't have an even number you will either have to take part yourself (though this makes it difficult to keep an eye on what's going on, and to keep to time) or you will have to appoint one person as 'the caller' who calls time and gives the instructions. Choose this 'odd person' before the group moves into circles, so they're specially chosen rather than being given a compensatory role.

Other things you can do with it

- Moving slowly round in concentric circles until the facilitator calls 'Stop' is another way of selecting partners for pair work.

- Do it without cards, asking for real opinions on a topic. Pairs may agree or disagree but should still take turns and feed back what they hear.

- The topic under discussion could be from real life, such as 'Talk about a time when someone needed your help and you gave it.' For this activity, participants take turns to share their experiences and demonstrate that they have heard what their partner said. Keep these personal topics light for this activity, unless you are working in a small ongoing group where there is a lot of trust and the participants have all had similar experiences in connection with the topic (see also **Talking and Listening** in the section on drama).

see page 130 MORE IDEAS

Relaxation, body focus and visualisation

Many young people have never learnt techniques for relaxing their bodies and minds, apart from falling asleep, but relaxation techniques can help to counter stress and give a young person a sense of control over their bodies and their responses to events. Practising these techniques can be helpful for most young people, but they are a particularly useful aspect of sessions on anger management, stress or exam preparation.

Examples

➡ *A young person who is very worried about a coming event is guided into a relaxed state and asked to remember a time they felt very calm and confident and imagine feeling like that again. The worker has already talked to them beforehand about a time when they felt confident, so they don't have to strain too hard to remember this whilst relaxed.*

➡ *A group working on substance abuse issues is encouraged to practise some basic Tai Chi moves, to help them become aware of their bodies and feel in control of themselves.*

The way it works

Relaxation may be an odd or even threatening idea for some young people, especially those who have had to learn to be vigilant and on their guard against violence, oppressive behaviour or loss. Practising martial arts moves can be a good way of introducing bodily focus in a way that increases the young person's sense of control and power. Yoga can also be beneficial for providing an internal rather than external focus, without losing control. Relaxation sessions could come at the end of such activities as a way of resting the body and mind. Participants may prefer to be seated, or they could lie on mats. They may shut their eyes if they feel comfortable about doing so. Most relaxation sessions involve a facilitator talking through a set of instructions. You should begin by asking participants to be aware of the pattern of their own breathing. If you speak slowly and gently it will usually help those who are breathing very fast to slow down without forcing the issue. Introduce a sensory focus, with instructions such as,' Be aware of any sounds you can hear close by you and far way' and gradually ask participants to clench and relax different muscle groups in turn, either working from the feet to the head and face or vice versa. You can occasionally remind them to let their breath come easily and comment on the fact that as their bodies become relaxed they may feel heavy, as if it they are sinking into the mat or chair.

Before you start a relaxation session, it can be helpful to ask the participants to think of a situation that makes them feel warm, calm and relaxed, such as lying on the beach in a sunny place. This will be different for everyone. During the relaxation, you could ask them to imagine or visualise themselves in their own private place of relaxation and focus on what it looks like, smells like, sounds like, and what they can see around them. When the relaxation session is coming to an end, ask them to find something in their special place that they can bring back with them when they return to the present moment. To bring them back to reality, warn them that it is time to start coming back to reality and ask them to notice their breathing again, and then to be aware of the sounds around them, and finally to open their eyes and have a good stretch and take their time about getting up again. Have pencils and paper handy and ask participants to draw the thing they brought back, without speaking. They can keep the drawing as a reminder of their special calm place.

Tips for using it:

- Have a supply of comfortable floor mats handy, and make sure the young people are warm enough, as their bodies will cool down as they lie still.

- If you want to have background music, choose music that is calm and unobtrusive. It's often better to have no music at all, and be able to focus on the surrounding sounds.

- There are relaxation tapes available, though it's often best to talk it through live, as you can guage the timing better.

- As far as possible, make sure you won't be interrupted or overlooked.

- Encourage young people to make their own tapes, for personal practice of these techniques.

- Don't do relaxation exercises straight after a heavy meal, as all the internal activity involved in digestion seems to get in the way of relaxing deeply.

Other things you can do with it

Recommend commercial tapes/CDs for use at home.

Diamond ranking

Diamond ranking is a prioritising activity. It generates discussion about choices whilst achieving a set of priorities within a fairly short time-frame. Introducing a time limit can help groups to get working together. Diamond ranking can also stimulate discussion about how decisions are made in groups and in society. It can be used with groups and individuals.

Examples

 A campaigning group is asked to write out nine targets for their campaign on separate sticky notes. They then rank the targets in a diamond shape with nine points (see diagram). The top card has the highest priority and the bottom card the lowest. In between the highest and lowest are a pair of equal ranking cards that have quite high priority, three cards with an equal, medium level priority, and another pair that have a priority slightly above the lowest. The group is given eight minutes to decide on the order of the cards. The aim is to help them clarify their main purpose.

HIGH

LOW

 A girl who has an eating disorder is working on ways to keep her body healthy and well nurtured. She writes up nine activities that she might enjoy and that would make her feel good. Her counsellor gives her three minutes to rank these in a nine-point diamond shape. Between them, they look at the possibility of the girl starting to include her top ranking activity into her lifestyle.

The way it works

You can use this any time a group or individual needs to decide on their priorities. The ideas can be written on sticky notes so they are easy to rearrange during discussion. This activity encourages young people to consider why one idea should have priority over another. It can illustrate, for instance, how difficult it can be for a group of people with different interests to come to a joint decision about spending a limited budget.

Tips for using it

- Use this when you need to make a decision between nine or more ideas. If there are more than nine possible ideas, some will have to be jettisoned or incorporated with others before the ranking begins.

- It's useful to display a template on the flip chart sheets, with nine squares in a diamond shape, so group members can grasp the idea of how to arrange their sticky notes.

- If you spray brown paper with Spray Mount, it will stay sticky for long enough to use sheets of non-sticky paper as cards and rearrange them many times.

- Add other rules such as giving one member of the group the power of veto. If they can state their reason, they can say no to the ranking agreed by the rest of the group and their decision is final. How does this feel for the veto holder? For the others? Is it fair? Is it ever like this in real life? In what circumstances might someone be given this power?

Other things you can do with it

Try this activity using other shapes as well as diamonds. What difference do other patterns, such as circles, make to the prioritising process?

Yes, no, maybe

This is a bit like continuum lines, but there are only three choices along the line and cards are used instead of people with the group aiming to reach agreement about which cards should go in which pile. It is a way of generating discussion amongst young people about issues that affect them. Unlike continuum lines, this includes an option for undecided responses.

Examples

 A health promotion worker has prepared two sets of identical cards on which he has written facts and myths about sex and sexual health. He divides the group into two. Each group has one set of cards with enough for everyone to have a few cards each. When it is their turn, each person reads what is on their card and places it on a pile marked 'fact' 'myth' or 'unsure'. When each person has placed a card, there is discussion about whether everyone agrees or whether they want to move the cards to different piles. When everyone is satisfied, the group moves on to the remaining cards and repeats the activity. When no cards are left, they compare results between the groups, discuss any issues arising and clarify misconceptions.

 During a discussion about neighbourhood and community rights and responsibilities, a 'yes, no, maybe' activity is used, with cards describing the behaviour of different community members, such as 'A young mother complains that a group of young people is too boisterous on the bus', or 'A group of teenagers skateboard in a busy street.' This time the piles are for 'acceptable behaviour', 'unacceptable behaviour' or 'unsure'. This will probably raise issues about who the behaviour is acceptable to and how agreements can be negotiated between different interest groups (see also **Charters and Bills of Rights** from the section on the written word).

see page 40
MORE IDEAS

© Trust for the Study of Adolescence 2005: Wavelength

The way it works

This activity may be based on 'facts' that have a right or wrong answer, or it may draw on opinions and attitudes within the group. The latter is likely to generate more heated discussion. You will need to prepare your cards carefully beforehand, with enough different statements to cover the main issues on this topic. Make sure each person has at least three cards each. Be very clear in your instructions, using labels to show where the three piles are to be put, and what they are called. Make sure discussion is a genuine sharing of opinions, rather than a row. Be clear about your aims. For example this type of activity could be part of a revision of the group agreement, or it could lead to a meeting with other interest groups in the community or neighbourhood.

Tips for using it

- *Keep the groups small or people may get bored. Four or five to each group works well.*

- *This can be a lengthy activity. Allow the discussion to develop, but move it on when it shows signs of becoming repetitious or stuck.*

Other things you can do with it

- Ask young people to write their own cards on a topic, making sure they balance them between those people are likely to agree with and disagree, and some that people will be less sure about.

Jigsaws

Jigsaw activities are a great equaliser. They indicate that everyone has an equal but different place in the big picture and underline a positive message about team work. Holding the pieces and finding out where they fit also helps to relieve self consciousness about engaging with the topic in question. Jigsaw activities can offer quieter members of the group an equal chance to talk and be listened to.

Examples

 During work with a group of young people who have experienced parental separation, everyone is given a blank jigsaw piece made from card. They each write a few words or draw symbols on their jigsaw piece, to represent their own feelings and experience in relation to the separation. In turn, everyone fits their puzzle piece, saying something about what they have written or drawn.

 A jigsaw activity is used for getting young people into groups. Everyone is given a coloured jigsaw piece. They write their name on it, find the others who have the same colour and make the jigsaw. This is now their group. They can keep their puzzle piece to use as a membership ticket in an ongoing group.

The way it works

For each jigsaw, take two pieces of card. Use one as the backing sheet and cut the other up into the right number of interlocking jigsaw pieces (according to how many people are in each group.) Make sure it's clear which side of the jigsaw pieces is the underside. Number the corners of the backing sheet, and number the corner of the jigsaw pieces to match. This creates a guide to placing the first pieces of the puzzle and avoids unnecessary confusion. If the young people are going to write or draw on the jigsaw pieces, ask them to do it on the upper side.

Tips for using it:

- When the puzzle is being put together, it's easier to start with the corner pieces.

- If the aim of the activity is to gather experiences and points of view on a topic, as in the first example, make a rule that no-one else can speak while the person fitting their piece is speaking.

- If you want to save the completed puzzles, or put them up on the wall, you'll need to have some adhesive to stick the pieces to the backing sheet.

- If the topic is quite personal, the activity can take some time and is best with a small group or groups where there is already an atmosphere of safety and trust.

Other things you can do with it

Use jigsaws as a summing up activity. Pieces are handed out at the end of the session and young people are invited to write one word, or draw something about the session on their piece, then fit it into the puzzle. The completed puzzle sums up the session.

Moving into groups

When young people are expected to get into groups or teams for activities, it can easily raise issues about acceptance and rejection. Free choice of groups can also mean that small cliques form within the groups, or that people stay with their friends and don't mix with others. For these reasons, many group leaders have developed different ways of dividing people into groups using random selection.

Examples

→ A *group divides into sixes by using magazine pictures pre-cut into six shapes. The pieces are given out randomly and the group members have to find the others whose pieces make up their whole picture (see also* **Jigsaws** *in this section).*

see page 100 MORE IDEAS

→ *The facilitator calls out the months of the year, in order and asks people to stand in line according to when their birthday falls. When the line is complete, the facilitator counts people off into groups.*

→ *A group of young people suggest as many names as they need groups. They write each of these names on slips of paper as many times as they need to match the number of people for each group. They put all these slips of paper in a bag. Everyone picks out a slip of paper and joins that group.*

→ *The group facilitator prepares a jar of sweets or other small goodies in different colours or types. She invites people to select a goody from the jar and join up with others who have chosen the same. Group members can then eat the goodies.*

The way it works

Use these activities whenever you need to divide the young people into groups. Some are quicker than others. The quickest way of selecting is just to count people off round the room. To avoid this resulting in the usual groups of friends, use the

1,2,3,4 method and then say 'all the ones' 'all the twos' and so on until you have four groups. If you use this method the young people need to be asked beforehand to remember their number when they are counted. Selection methods that involve people mingling in order to find the others in their group take longer but can be beneficial at the start of a group working together. You may want to choose methods that deliberately separate some people who distract each other too much, or put together people who haven't worked together at all. With random methods you can't control the outcome.

Tips for using it

- Remember that there may be resistance to methods that split people up or encourage people to work with someone they don't like.

- Try to be aware of any bullying going on in the group. One group member may be afraid of working with certain others. This doesn't mean you shouldn't try it, but be prepared to monitor the situation closely.

- However much you prepare, you will often be left with odd numbers in a group, or not enough people for pairs. Consider how to adapt your activities to awkward numbers.

- Vary your selection processes, or those who want to work together all the time will learn to engineer the result they want.

- In the initial stages of group work, try to vary the small groups and pairs as much as possible.

Other things you can do with it

- Use a moving into groups activity as an ice-breaker or warm up activity at the beginning of a session.

- See also **Moving Circles** in this section.

see page 92
MORE IDEAS

Dot voting

Dot voting is a way of visually representing the range of views in the group at any time. It can be used as a way of evaluating learning, or for deciding on priorities or taking action.

Examples

 After charting up quick thoughts on possible activities for future sessions, a youth worker facilitates a group of young people to rearrange the ideas they have come up with, so that similar ideas are grouped together, by joint consent. Each of these new sets, pairs or separate ideas is given a heading, agreed by the group. The headings are written up separately. Group members are then given three coloured dots each. At a given signal they all stick their dots on the idea-headings they most want to take action on, prioritising three. Some headings now have more votes than others. These activities are prioritised for the immediate future sessions and the group decides what they want to do about the suggestions that got fewer votes.

 At the start of a session on healthy eating, the facilitator draws a line in the middle of a flipchart sheet and writes 'I know a lot about this subject' at the top of the sheet. At one end of the line she writes 'I agree' and at the other end, 'I disagree'. She asks the group to stick a coloured dot at the point on the line that most suits their current knowledge on the subject. This sheet is then taken down until the end of the session, At the end of the session, a similar sheet is drawn up with the same heading and the same instructions are followed. The group compares the two charts and discusses any changes.

10

The way it works

You need lots of strips of coloured dots. Dot voting is a bit like **Continuum Lines** in this section, but this variation means the results can be recorded and kept for comparison with later votes. To avoid dominant group members leading the vote, all participants should stick up their dots simultaneously, after a few minutes have been given for everyone to decide where they are going to put them. Dot voting can help group members to decide on priorities or to evaluate their learning, as in the examples given.

see page 90
MORE IDEAS

Tips for using it

- You can use different shapes, for example smiley or frowning faces, for different purposes.

- Take care that smaller voices don't get marginalised. Find other ways of making priorities and decisions as well as dot voting.

- If you ask for quick thoughts to be written on sticky notes and stuck onto the board, they can be rearranged into groups easily later.

Other things you can do with it

- Use this as a way of starting discussion about voting methods, and their relative fairness and democracy in general.

Board games

Commercial educational board games usually aim to introduce information, challenge myths and raise topics for discussion. They have a recommended age range and supporting materials for the facilitator. Some are well designed and combine a fun activity with an increase in knowledge on a subject. However, you might want to think about creating your own game with a group, as part of the learning involved in a topic.

Examples

➡ *A group creates their own trivia type game on the subject of careers, using four different knowledge areas appropriate counters and question and answer cards within each area.*

➡ *A young men's group creates a game where players move round the board landing occasionally on feelings cards or opinion cards. When they do, they have to pick up a card and answer the question truthfully giving their opinion about something, or saying how something makes them feel.*

➡ *A class of pupils working on alcohol and health creates a snakes and ladders game. Together they agree on suggestions for what would take players down the snakes or up the ladders.*

The way it works

Decide on the aim of your board game. For example board games may be aimed at generating discussion and challenging attitudes, or increasing knowledge about a subject. Ask the group for examples of board games, or bring in some of your own. These can be used as basic formats to follow. You will probably need some stiff

card, paper, coloured pens and glue. You will also need to decide what you are going to use as counters. These should be in keeping with the topic. Small record cards can be used as question or instruction cards if needed. Large groups can be split into smaller groups and pairs, each with a specific task towards making the game. Remember to give the game a name and pilot its use.

Tips for using it

- Consider how many people can play the game at once. This is usually quite a small number, or the game becomes boring because each person has to wait too long for their turn.

- Try to make the layout and the counters used tie in with the theme.

- Keep up-to-date with quiz games on television. They may help you think of a format for a group game.

Other things you can do with it

- Games don't always have to have specific answers on the cards. You can have a set of blank cards, for instance labelled 'help' and 'hindrance'. Then when a person lands on a particular choice or dilemma described on the board, they are allowed one of each card. They must write on each card what would help or hinder them and then move on when their turn comes round again.

- Games don't always need boards. You can make a giant game space that gets people moving physically. Laminate some large paper squares and form a circle with them on the floor. Some are blank, some are labelled 'O' and some 'F.' Also prepare hand-held cards labelled 'OPINION' and 'FACT'. The players in turn roll a large sponge dice into the circle. If it lands on 'F' they pick up a 'FACT' card and must answer the question. If they land on 'O' they answer an 'OPINION' question. This game can be useful for sessions on sex and relationships, drugs and alcohol or other health, equality or environmental issues.

Communicating through drama

The use of drama can increase communication skills and self confidence in young people, deepen empathy and enhance team work. It can also be a powerful way of raising awareness about issues and developing problem-solving skills for dilemmas young people face in their every day lives. It is largely a social process and most of these ideas work well with groups, though many can also be adapted to one to one work. Minority groups who have experienced discrimination, or whose perspectives have not been heard or valued, often feel particularly empowered by drama activities. Whilst it is important to plan drama activities to accommodate different needs and abilities in a group, it is also worth remembering that people with specific impairments, disabilities and communication difficulties may benefit enormously from the opportunity to express themselves through drama.

Contents

1. Forum theatre
2. Freeze the scene
3. Hot seating
4. The angel and the demon
5. Sculpting
6. Role play or practice exercises
7. Snapshots – sound and vision
8. Rehearsal for life
9. Making a video
10. One group one mind one body
11. Talking and listening
12. Non-verbal language

Forum theatre

Forum theatre uses performance and workshop techniques to help young people examine choices that lead to problems. Alternative choices can be suggested by the audience and tried out by the actors, or by audience members. Many theatre-in-education groups use forum theatre, but workers can use it themselves with groups. Different techniques can be incorporated, some of which are described in more detail on the following pages.

Examples

➤ *A school asks a theatre in education company to come and present a forum theatre performance and workshop on the subject of teenage pregnancy. The theatre company is one that is known to tour an effective piece on this subject.*

➤ *A group works on developing and rehearsing a scenario in which the main protagonist is a young woman recently released from a Youth Offenders Institution after serving time for dealing heroin. She is tagged and on curfew. She meets up with her old friends for the first time since she was sentenced. Most of her friends use or sell drugs. They are pleased to see her and assume she will still be part of their group. The scenario explores the young woman's conflicting feelings and potential responses to this situation.*

The way it works

Divide your large group into smaller groups of about six people. Try to make sure that people who do not want to perform are evenly distributed amongst the groups. They can have roles as directors of the scene. Using prepared scenario cards or the group's own ideas, ask each group to plan and rehearse a short scene that illustrates the issue the whole group is working on. The scene should be acted out by a main character or 'protagonist', whose choices are the main focus of the drama. There should also be one or more 'antagonists' in the scene, who make it hard for the protagonist to make a healthy choice, and the protagonist might also have a friend or supportive family member. The scene should lead the protagonist through a series of 'faulty' choices towards a final desperate dilemma, which is where the scene ends. At this point, the dilemma should not be resolved. When each group has planned and rehearsed their scene, bring the groups back together to act out their scenes for each other, uninterrupted.

For the next stage a note-taker should be appointed. Each scene is then played again using stop-start techniques in which the audience may call out 'STOP' or 'FREEZE' whenever they see a possibility for the protagonist to behave differently towards a positive outcome. The audience member who stops the action suggests a different way for the protagonist to behave and the group acts out this new suggestion, checking with the audience member that they have understood and are acting correctly. This change and its possible consequences are noted and the scene proceeds until someone calls it to a halt again. By the end of the scene, the note-taker will have charted up a selection of alternative choices and the whole group can discuss these choices further before moving on to the next group's presentation of their scene.

see page
112, 114, 116
MORE IDEAS

Techniques such as **Freeze the Scene, Hot Seating** and **The Angel and the Demon** (all in this section) are examples of techniques that may be part of forum theatre work.

Tips for using it

- *Remember this is problem-solving drama, not psychodrama or dramatherapy. Don't let it get too personal. Avoid having someone who has experienced a particular situation act out the role they played in real life.*

- *Use a warm up activity before starting a drama activity.*

- *Use a ritual for getting in and out of role. (**see Role Play or Practice Exercises** in this section) This may feel odd but it is very important. Acting a character can become very real and the actors need a way of stepping back from the emotional charge of playing a role.*

see page 120
MORE IDEAS

- *In preparing their scenes, group members should be clear about who the characters are. What has brought them into this situation, what sort of people are they and what relationship do they have with each other?*

Other things you can do with it

- The Brazilian theatre director Augusto Boal, on whose work forum theatre is based called the audience the spectactors because he encouraged them to get up on stage and take the role of the protagonst to demonstrate their suggestion as to how the character should act. This can be very empowering, but wait until you feel confident in facilitating it this way.

Freeze the scene

This technique involves stopping the action of a scenario in order to understand what is going on for the characters involved at a particular point. It can be used in role play activities, forum theatre or when watching a video.

Examples

 In a forum theatre scene, the tension is mounting. The odds are stacked against the protagonist and she doesn't know which way to turn. The facilitator calls 'freeze' and the players stop the action, whilst remaining in character. The facilitator taps a character on the shoulder and asks the audience a relevant question such as, 'What is this character feeling now?' 'What would he like to say?' or 'What does he want to do?' The same can be done with the other characters. And then at the call of 'unfreeze' the action moves on. Exploration of the characters' thoughts and feelings helps understand their later actions.

 Whilst watching an educational video drama, the facilitator pauses the tape or disc and asks for comments on what's going on for the actors and how the audience can tell. This should lead to discussion of body language and other ways of showing what a character is feeling. It may be that the character's feelings are obvious because they are behaving in the opposite way, or because they are not doing something, rather than because they are.

The way it works

Freezing the scene in drama, whether it's live drama or on TV, can work as a reminder that people are always making choices and it's possible to create a little bit of time for reflection in between a thought and an act. Young people can learn to freeze the scene in their own heads, for example, rather than being triggered

into a fight. This technique can help to tease out the relationship between thoughts, feelings and behaviours. Many young people respond to situations so quickly that they are not even aware of any difference between thoughts, feelings and actions, or that there is any time available to make a conscious decision.

Tips for using it

- *Instead of speaking, the facilitator can hold up cards behind the chosen players, to ask for ideas about their thoughts (a thought bubble) feelings (a heart) and what they want to do (a stick person). This acts as an additional visual reminder of these elements in decision-making.*

Other things you can do with it

- Once the convention is established, audience members could be the ones to shout 'freeze' when they want to explore why a character is acting as they are. It's usually best to play a scene through uninterrupted first though, or the tension of the drama may be spoilt for the audience.

- The freeze the scene technique can be combined with **Hot Seating** (described next in this section).

see page 114 **MORE IDEAS**

Hot seating

Hot seating isn't easy, but young people can enjoy rising to the challenge. It encourages deeper exploration of the experiences or knowledge of one person, or one role play character at a time. Groups enjoy the freedom to be creative and wide-ranging in their questioning.

Examples

→ *In a small group discussion, one chair is left empty. At any time, any group member can voluntarily go and sit in this 'hot seat' and be asked questions by the others about the topic being discussed. The others must give full attention to the person in the hot seat.*

→ *After a role play activity, one character sits in the hot seat. He stays 'in character' as the rest of the group ask questions such as,'What does it feel like to be in this situation?' 'Why did you tell (another character) to go away?'.*

The way it works

The hot seat is the name for activities where one person is put on the spot and asked questions by the others. If the person is taking part in a role play activity, they should stay in character and try to think how that character would answer the questions. It can be a very useful way of finding out more about that character, to enrich the learning from the role play. Both the audience and the character themselves often find out more than they realised they would.

If the hot seat is part of a general group discussion, as in the first example above, anyone can sit on it at any time. This may allow them to demonstrate their knowledge or experience of a subject, or it might enable them to talk about a personal experience they wouldn't begin to talk about unless they were questioned by others.

Tips for using it

- People can get deeply into their role play character through hot seating and it's important to have a ritual for debriefing and returning to their own personality afterwards (See **Role Play or Practice Exercises** in this section).

see page 120
MORE IDEAS

- In a general discussion group that doesn't involve role play, using the hot seat can become a bit like a truth or dare game, and generate the same level of risk and excitement. Make sure you keep this safe for the participants. It's best not to use this technique when discussing very personal or emotional issues unless the group is very used to working together in this way and you're used to working with them.

Other things you can do with it

- During a role play activity, encourage observers to stop the action at any time by shouting out 'hot seat' and nominate the character they want to ask a question. For example they might want to know why that character just behaved a certain way or said a particular thing (See also **Freeze the Scene** in this section).

see page 112
MORE IDEAS

The angel and the demon

Many of us have warring voices inside our heads, giving us contradictory advice. One voice tells us to do something we know isn't good for us, while the other warns us off, or one voice criticises everything we do, while the other says we're okay as we are. The angel and the demon externalises this phenomenon so these contradictory sides of ourselves become easier to examine and control.

Examples

 A girls' group is using forum theatre to focus on self-esteem issues. One group acts out a dilemma at a party. The main character is a girl who has low self-esteem. On the day of the party she has come out in spots. Her friends persuade her to go to the party despite her desire to stay at home and hide. The person she fancies arrives at the party. The facilitator freezes the action at this point and asks all the characters except the girl to move aside. The facilitator invites two volunteers to become the girl's 'angel' and 'demon'. They sit on each side of the girl and argue their case while the girl stays quiet. The angel promotes a positive perspective on the situation and the demon is negative. Each suggests a different course of action. The facilitator suggests that the girl asks the audience which one she should pay attention to, and why. Based on this decision, the scenario continues with the other players while the two volunteers return to the audience.

The way it works

This can be used in conjunction with forum theatre to illustrate the opposing voices that may be in a person's head when they have to make a decision. The facilitator freezes the scene at a key choice point, and asks the protagonist what different thoughts are going on. With the help of volunteers from the audience, opposing thoughts are characterised as 'angel' and 'demon.' The angel and demon may argue with each other, or engage in a dialogue with the protagonist, or with the audience. The demon may encourage the character to take the easy way out of the situation – the way they usually take that gets them nowhere in the end. The angel may encourage the character to try something different. As in a TV game show, the protagonist can ask for an audience vote to decide which path to choose. Unfreeze the scene and let the charcters act out this scenario with the ending suggested by the audience. Was it the best choice?

Use this as a springboard, not only for discussion about the decision in the scene, but for discussion about how people deal with dealing with warring thoughts in their heads. Are they always so clear cut? How do people know which one is the angel and which the demon? How do they decide which one to take notice of? Where do these voices come from?

Tips for using it

- Don't use this activity if a young person in the group has difficulty distinguishing between voices in the head and voices in the 'real world.'

Other things you can do with it

- In individual work you could adapt this as a visual activity, drawing the angel and the demon and giving them speech bubbles to fill in. Or you could invite a young person to choose miniature animals, stones or bean bags to represent these different voices and describe what they say.

Sculpting

Live sculpting can give a vivid picture of how different factors affect a situation or a set of relationships. It can also demonstrate how change might look and feel. Young people who are nervous about drama activities often find sculpting less threatening, as their part is more prescribed.

Examples

 A young man uses live sculpting to work on an action plan towards his goal of going to college. He asks for volunteers to represent him and his goal. He positions this pair as far away from each other as he feels the goal to be from himself. Next, he invites volunteers to take the part of the obstacles he thinks will get in between himself and his goal and he puts these people in place accordingly. Then he considers the people and other resources that can help him and volunteers step into the positions he chooses until there are more helping resources than obstacles. The young man assesses and rearranges this sculpt until it resembles reality for him. Before the sculpt dissolves, he decides on the first step of his action plan, involving making use of one or more of his most accessible resources to get nearer to the goal.

 In an anger management session, two groups are given five minutes to arrange themselves into two still images or 'tableaux,' one representing anger and the other representing sadness. Each group shows their tableau to the other for comments and discussion.

5

The way it works

Group sculpts are time consuming but everybody can be involved and can learn from one situation being sculpted out. This is a technique used in therapy, but unless you have proper training, it's best to stick to using sculpts for problem-solving and expressing ideas and feelings, rather than for deeper exploration of, for instance, a current family situation. You don't need any dialogue in a sculpt, though you could combine it with **Hot Seating** (also in this section).

see page 114
MORE IDEAS

Tips for using it

- As with any role play work, the people involved should use a ritual for going in and out of role, even if they aren't strictly 'acting' a part (see also **Role Play or Practice Exercises** in this section).

see page 120
MORE IDEAS

- When using group sculpts to create tableaux on a theme, encourage the group to work quickly and to have the aim of communicating an idea to the others.

Other things you can do with it

- You can use the same principle when working with individuals, using stones or other objects instead of people (see **Symbolic Objects** in the section on moving sorting and handling).

see page 88
MORE IDEAS

Role play or practice exercises

These offer a way of viewing a situation from a different perspective, or rehearsing a situation the young person is likely to find herself in. Role play can be used to practise skills such as mentoring, with one person playing the mentee and one the mentor, or to re-enact a situation and explore how it could be done differently. This use is very similar to forum theatre.

Examples

→ During a session on assertiveness training, three young people are given character cards that have a description of a character and how they usually behave in a conflict situation. One character's behaviour is passive, one aggressive and one assertive. The group facilitator tells the group to interact with each other at a bus stop on a rainy day when there is not enough room in the shelter for all three. After rehearsal, this situation is acted out for the others in the group, who should be able to guess which character is playing which type of behaviour. The scenario stimulates discussion about these behaviours and their possible consequences.

→ A trainee peer mentor role plays a situation where a mentee is visiting for the first time. The mentee is given notes on how to behave so that the mentor can practise specific skills in response.

The way it works

Use warm up exercises to relieve self-consciousness before using role play. Some people enjoy role play more than others and are quicker to volunteer. Don't force anyone to get involved if they are not ready, but do find a role for them in the group, for example helping to direct or sculpt the scene, or observing with critical feedback. Role play is particularly useful in training assertiveness and in working on bullying. Those who have been victimised can find it empowering and enlightening to role play being a bully.

Tips for using it

- Take care in setting up role play scenarios. Explain clearly what the situation is, who the characters are, and what is expected of them. Make sure everyone understands the aim of the role play and be prepared to offer directions if needed.

- Always use a ritual for coming in and out of role play. It can be as simple as each person saying their own name and then the name of the character they are about to play, and then reversing this at the end. It is important to find a technique that works for the group and always use it so that no-one in the group confuses the person with the role they are playing.

- Sometimes people get carried away with their role and create too many difficulties for the main character, so they cannot win. Point out to the group if this is beginning to happen.

- Always leave time for discussion after a role play. This also gives time for the participants to get back to being themselves. Make sure discussion relates to the characters in the role play, not the people who played those characters.

Other things you can do with it

- Role play or practice exercises can be used to rehearse situations such as job interviews.

Snapshots - sound and vision

These are useful activities for helping groups to work together, and for developing observation and communication skills through sound, spatial awareness and physical expression. These activities can also be used as warm-ups before acting out more complex scenarios.

Examples

 A group working on community safety creates snapshots of safe and unsafe areas within their neighbourhood at different times of the day or week. These snapshots become the basis for developing improvised dramas that take place in these settings. This helps young people to express how they feel about safety in their community and suggest changes they would like to see.

The way it works

Divide the group into smaller groups of about six or seven. Give each group a setting that's familiar to them such as 'at the beach' 'at the swimming pool' or 'on the train.' Choose settings that have identifiable sounds as well as being visually recognisable. Ask each group for 'quick thoughts' about the scene (see **Quick Thoughts** in the section on the written word). What would they see in this setting? What sounds would they hear – close up? – in the distance? What would people be doing in these settings? What makes this setting different from other places? Give them a few minutes to create a snapshot of this setting. To make a snapshot they arrange themselves in a group tableau (see **Sculpting** in this section) that represents and characterises their setting, and provide a sound track by mimicking sounds from this setting. They may need to move a little to make the sounds, but essentially they should be still rather than moving around.

When the groups are ready, each performs their snapshot for the others, who try to guess what the setting is and how they recognised it, or made other assumptions.

see page 42
MORE IDEAS

see page 118
MORE IDEAS

Tips for using it

- Stress that although the audience may interpret the scene differently from the way the players intended, this does not make them wrong. What the audience sees might be something that the group represented without realising it. This is an important lesson to learn about communication generally. Sometimes we don't send out the message as clearly as we could, but even when we do, other factors affect the way the receiver interprets this message.

- Encourage the players to listen to the feedback and interpretations from the audience without saying anything. Then ask them what they remember about what was said. This is useful pratice for accepting feedback generally. After that, they can add comments of their own if they wish.

Other things you can do with it

- If you want to explore a theme by developing one of the snapshots further, you could begin with one of the characters in the snapshot. Ask the audience who they think this character is. Give him or her some detailed characteristics, then explore what she is doing there. Where has she come from and what does she want? Develop another character in the same way. This is the character who stands in the way of the first character getting what she wants. Now you have the basis of a little dramatic story and the players can start to improvise the scene.

Rehearsal for life

This is useful for building confidence in dealing with a daunting or unfamiliar situation such as an important interview or meeting, or for trying out changes to a negative situation. A young person plays themselves in a real-life situation, with one or more others taking the other roles. This method suits work with individuals or small supportive groups. It can increase young people's confidence in behaving in new ways.

Examples

 A young woman wants to change a situation in which someone is pressurising her into doing things she doesn't want to do. She talks with a worker about this situation, and comes up with a number of alternative responses to this pressure. The worker encourages the young woman to be creative in thinking up more and more alternatives. The worker then takes the role of the other person and the young woman tries out one of the alternatives. Stepping out of role again, the worker gives feedback. They try the same response again until it feels familiar and continue this pattern with other alternatives.

 A young man rehearses an important phone call. He talks it through with his foster carer in advance and is encouraged to think about what he wants to get from the call, what responses he might get and whether a phone call is the best approach to make at this stage. The foster carer helps him to consider how he will remember what is said in the phone call and how he might deal with what is said. After discussion, the foster carer offers to rehearse the phone call with the young man.

The way it works

This activity needs detailed preparation. You need to understand the situation from the young person's perspective before you can approach the rehearsal. You also need to bear in mind how the other person might respond. Help the young person to come up with ideas for different ways of handling the situation. As far as possible these suggestions should come from the young person, but you could add some suggestions of your own. When you are sure you understand the situation, go ahead with the rehearsal. Afterwards, give feedback to the young person. If you are working in a small group, others in the group can be involved in feedback or in role playing the other person. Make sure you have something encouraging to say as well as any suggestions for improvements. Check out how they feel at each stage of the rehearsal. Offer to give them some time to talk about it after they have dealt with the situation in real life.

Tips for using it

- This may make a young person feel self-conscious. Acknowledge this but encourage them to try it. If they really don't want to role play, you can still discuss alternative techniques with them and ask them to pratice them on their own.

- Don't get too far into your role in these scenes. Focus on a couple of exchanges at a time and be very clear about stepping into and out of role.

Other things you can do with it

- You could use this technique for a detailed rehearsal of an important interview. If you have access to a video camera, it can be useful for the young person to assess themselves, and for the worker to detail specific points.

- A small group could use this activity for rehearsing come-back lines to put-downs they have experienced. Use the group's creativity to develop a range of come-back lines, and give feedback jointly as individuals rehearse.

Making a video

Young people can find it empowering to take control of this familiar medium and use it to express their own views, feelings or research on a topic. Working towards a concrete product can motivate them to work together as a group. You may need to hire in outside expertise and technology and there are now many organisations who provide these services in community settings.

Examples

 A youth centre is to be closed down. A group of young people makes a video that involves showing the centre in use. They interview the centre users and the decision makers who want to close it. They organise a screening of the video at the centre and invite the decision makers.

 A young disabled woman with communication difficulties is moving into independent housing. She makes a video film about her care needs, so that different assistants will be able to understand what she wants without her needing to repeat complicated instructions with each change of personnel.

The way it works

Obviously you need to have some basic equipment and expertise. There are several clear stages involved in making a video. First you need to be clear about why you are using video. What do you want to say and how do you want to say it? How much research or preparation have you done already? Is video a useful way of communicating what you want? Is the film's story or message best conveyed in documentary style or drama, or a combination of both?

Decide beforehand where and when the film is to be shown, and to whom. What skills does the group have already? What help is needed? Your plan should include a breakdown of the stages involved and who will be responsible for them. Some aspects of the process will need more skills training than others. Video making offers the possibility for young people to draw on skills they didn't realise they had. There are lots of different roles involved and all group members should be able to be involved somehow. Keep an eye on the group process throughout. Encourage the less involved and make sure the more enthusiastic don't take over. Deal with conflict as it arises and be confident that conflict is normal when people are really committed to a group project. Acknowledge all the hard work that went into the making and affirm the learning involved.

Tips for using it

- *Enjoy the finished product. Can you think of more uses for it, or ways the young people can develop their new skills and pass them on to others?*

Other things you can do with it

- Fund raise for your own video equipment or, given the rapid developments in film and video technology, begin a fund from which to hire equipment when you need it in the future.

One group, one mind, one body

This is any drama activity that encourages group members to focus on each other to the extent that they can move and even talk as if with one mind. These activities are an excellent way of increasing concentration, physical awareness and team building.

Example

 A group forms a circle and everyone takes off one shoe and keeps it close to them. One person throws their shoe across the circle to someone else who passes it on until everyone has caught and thrown the shoe. This is repeated, following the same pattern of throwing and catching, until there is a good rhythm going and everyone knows who to catch from and throw to. Then another person throws their shoe into the circle, following the same pattern. This process is repeated until there is a circle of flying shoes, with everybody tightly focused on each other and on the rhythm of catching and throwing.

The way it works

These activities involve a physical or vocal action that is performed at the same time as, or in immediate response to, another person or a group of people. The aim is to practise these movements and sounds until those practising experience an almost telepathic connection with the others – a sense that they are moving to the same rhythm. You can think up ideas of your own, but as a starter, here are some ideas that work:

● THE SQUEEZE. Hold hands in a circle. Explain that you are going to pass a 'squeeze' round the circle and that as each person feels the squeeze with one hand, they should pass it on with the other. Then squeeze the hand of the person on your right. Carry on with this until the group is really concentrating. There are usually some accidental false squeezes along the way. You can also do this activity using clapping. Speed it up and pass it round the circle until it is almost a continuous sound.

● QUICK SHAPES. Ask the group to move randomly round the room in different directions. Explain that you will call out the name of a shape and without words, they must quickly arrange themselves in this shape. Start with easy shapes such as a square or a triangle, and move to more difficult ones like the letter 'S' or 'W'.

● ONE VOICE. Start with a small group. Tell them that you are going to ask them some simple questions, to which they must respond in whole sentences (For example, 'What's your name?' 'My name is …'). Don't tell them what to say, just that they must answer as if they are one person. No single person leads or follows, and if you see someone doing this, ask them to start again. They must be so focussed on each other that they are able to open their mouths and come out with the same words. They should stand very close to each other and all be able to see all the others. Now ask them some questions and let them reply.

Tips for using it

- When the group has practised 'one voice' they can move into two groups and be two separate people having a conversation. Give them a set up, such as 'your first date'.

Other things you can do with it

• These activities can also be done in pairs, for instance facing each other as if in a full length mirror. Each pair should slowly move arms, hands, legs, heads and bodies in the mirror, but neither knows who is the mirror and who the real person. Or two people can talk with one voice to another pair.

Talking and listening

This includes any activity aimed at increasing awareness of communication skills and practising them. Talking and listening skills are often included in training such as peer mentoring or mediation. This type of skills practice often includes an observer giving feedback on the skills.

Example

 In peer mediation training, two people are given a scenario card detailing the conflict that has brought them to the mediation session and how they currently feel about each other. A third person plays the mediator and a fourth observes the listening skills of the mediator as they try to help the couple. After the role play, everyone moves out of role. The observer gives feedback to the mediator. The mediator repeats what the observer says without commenting. The warring couple then give feedback on the mediator's skills and he repeats this. At the end, he makes his own comments about his skills. The facilitator makes sure he has heard the positive comments, not just the negative ones. No-one is allowed to criticise the 'performance' of the couple – the feedback is just about how well the mediator listened.

The way it works

Some talking and listening activities focus specifically on skills practice, but it is also important to have plenty of discussion about what helps and hinders communication generally, as the intent, context and relationship are as important as the skills themselves. Young people recognise this instinctively. Talking and listening skills activities should heighten their awareness and increase their confidence, rather than making them feel deskilled because they can't name different skills correctly. It's okay for people to have different styles as long as they stick to certain principles to do with the purpose of their communication and the boundaries of the relationship. Here are some activities you could use:

● BLOCKS TO LISTENING. Ask the group to think of times when people don't listen to them properly – what is it they do instead? Write down these suggestions, which may include, for example 'they want to get in with their own opinion' or 'they look at me as if I'm stupid' or 'they finish my sentences for me'. The group moves into threes. Each threesome chooses one of the suggestions on the list. One becomes the talker, trying to tell the others about an accident they've just witnessed. The others exhibit the chosen listening block. Give them a couple of minutes to rehearse, then ask for volunteers to show their scenario to the others in the group. Did they demonstrate the block accurately? How did the talker feel?

● SITTING ON HANDS. Move into pairs or small groups. Discuss something everyone can join in on. The group talks for two minutes but they must sit on their hands. Ask for feedback on how this affected their conversation. Do the same using the instruction to avoid eye contact, or to keep eye contact but maintain a neutral facial expression.

● SAY NOTHING. In pairs, the talker talks for a minute while the other person listens without saying anything in words, though they may show they are listening in other ways. At the end of the minute, the listener should try to sum up the main points of what the talker said. How did that feel for the talker? For the listener?

After using these activities, ask the group what they think makes a good listener. How does a good listener demonstrate that they are listening?

Tips for using it

- Give them topics of conversation to start them off, but remind them that the purpose is to talk and listen. They can feel free to stray from the subject.

- Focus on the qualities of good listeners as well as the skills.

- Model being a good listener generally.

- Encourage discussion about what sometimes makes it hard to talk and how people deal with things they can't talk about.

Other things you can do with it

- Watch videos of people talking and listening in dramas and chat shows. Encourage the group to pick out some of the skills and principles they have worked on.

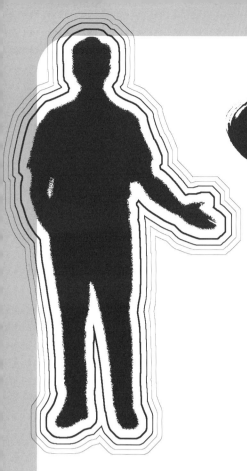

Non verbal language

This includes any activity that focuses on non-verbal communication such as body language, interpersonal space, intonation, appearance, facial expression, pace and pitch of speech. These cues affect the way we interpret other people's behaviour and personality, and the way they interpret ours. Non-verbal language activities may overlap with **Talking and Listening, Forum Theatre** and other activities from this section.

see pages 130, 110 **MORE IDEAS**

Example

 Working in pairs, young people talk to each other for one minute in gibberish. The gibberish sounds like a language but does not include any real words. Afterwards, they give feedback about whether they could understand each other at all. Some of the pairs perform their conversation for the whole group and there is discussion about what helped the pair understand each other or not. The group then divides into groups of four. In turn, each person in the group tells a joke in gibberish. The others laugh at the punch line. Afterwards they discuss how they could tell it was the punch line and what made it recognisable as a joke.

The way it works

There are many activities for observing and practising non-verbal language. Here are some examples:

● SPATIAL AWARENESS. In pairs, one young person is the talker and the other the listener. The talker sits in a chair and talks for one minute on an easy topic such as my favourite popstar or television programme. The listener doesn't respond verbally, but moves around as the talker is talking, sometimes standing close, sometimes further away, sometimes sitting, sometimes facing their partner, sometimes behind them or at their side. Afterwards, ask the talkers how they felt. Did any of the positions feel more comfortable than others? Now do the same activity with the roles reversed. Any additional comments?

12

● FACIAL EXPRESSIONS. Write the names of some facial expressions on separate large pieces of card. Add an 'emoticon' type face showing that expression. Ask for a volunteer from the group. The volunteer faces the others. Stand behind the volunteer and hold up one of the cards so the group can see, but the volunteer can't. The whole group show the chosen expression on their faces. The volunteer guesses the emotion. Swap volunteers and do it again as much as you want to. This is a quick, fun activity. Ask for comments about how easy it is to know what a person is really feeling. How else do we guess as well as by their face?

● GUESS WHAT'S HAPPENING. Move the group into pairs. Give each pair a scenario on a card. For example, 'You have just had an argument' or 'One of you **is trying to persuade the other to do something they don't want to do.' Give the** pairs a minute to show this scenario as a still image, using body language. The pairs show their images to the others who guess what's happening (see also **Snapshots - Sound and Vision** in this section).

see page 122
MORE IDEAS

Tips for using it

- Encourage young people to watch out for non-verbal language going on around them and on television. Are they aware of how their own non-verbal language affects others?

- Young people will have lots of understanding of non-verbal language but they may not have had the opportunity to discuss it before. This can raise issues about how to respond when someone's non-verbal language makes you feel uncomfortable.

Other things you can do with it

- Use these activities in assertiveness training.

Further resources and suppliers

Further resources and suppliers

Although some excellent resources for working with young people are commercially available, your budget may be tight and you want to know you are getting value for money. The following questions may help you to evaluate available resources:

- What is the purpose of this resource?

- Does it achieve its purpose?

- Is it all in one format, such as worksheets, or does it mix a few different formats together? Is this what you are looking for?

- Is it right for your age group? Is it user-friendly for them?

- Is it for groups or individuals?

- How often would you use it?

- How interactive is it?

- How inclusive is it?

- Are there any limitations or cautions about using this resource?

- Can you adapt it yourself and find other ways of using it?

- Is it worth the money?

- Are there accompanying notes with resources such as videos?

Selected resources

The following books were particularly helpful in the preparation of this handbook.

Brody, R. (1998) *Getting Through, Young People and Communication*, Trust for the Study of Adolescence (TSA)

Catan, L. (2004) *Becoming Adult: changing youth transitions in the 21st century*, Trust for the Study of Adolescence (TSA)

Geldard, K. and Geldard, D. (2004) *Counselling Adolescents: the pro-active approach*, SAGE

Lee, S. Muhammad, F.T. and Downes, R. (2002) *Listening in Colour, creating a meeting place with young people*, Trust for the Study of Adolescence (TSA)

McConville, B. (2002) *Where to Look for Help: A guide for parents and carers of teenagers,* Trust for the Study of Adolescence (TSA)

Melia, J. and McGowan, M. (2002) *Working with Young People, developing professional practice in interpersonal, communication and counselling skills,* Trust for the Study of Adolescence (TSA)

Taylor, A. (2003) *Responding to Adolescents – Helping relationship skills for youth workers, mentors and other advisors,* Russell House Publishing

Suppliers

The following list is not comprehensive, but includes some of the main organisations that produce resources for working with young people. We have selected suppliers that stock a range of materials such as training packs, board games, CD-ROMs, videos and DVDs as well as books.

TSA's publication *Where to Look for Help – a guide for parents and carers of teenagers* includes the details of a wide number of national organisations, many of which provide resources for parents and professionals.

British Institute of Learning Disabilities (BILD)
Booksource, 32 Finlas Street, Cowlairs Estate, Glasgow, G22 5DU
08702 402182
0141 5570189 (fax)
www.bild.org.uk

BILD has a range of books, training materials and they also publish a series of books for people with learning disabilities on topics that include coping with stress, alcohol and sex.

Heinemann
The Order Department, Freepost (OF1771) PO Box 381, Oxford OX2 8BR
01865 888080
01865 314029 (fax)
www.heinemann.co.uk
email: orders@heinemann.co.uk

Heinemann is an educational publisher that produces curriculum resources for both primary and secondary schools. The resources include books, CD-ROMs, photocopiable material and training packs. The *What's an issue* series in the PSHE/Citizenship section covers many subjects including prejudice, relationships, drugs and families.

Incentive Plus Ltd
PO Box 5220, Great Horwood, Milton Keynes MK17 0YN
01908 526120
01908 526130 (fax)
www.incentiveplus.co.uk
email: orders@incentiveplus.co.uk

The Incentive Plus catalogue has a comprehensive range of products such as CD-ROM games, CD-ROM classroom resources, board games, posters, videos, books and teachers photocopy manuals. Subjects include anti-bullying, self-esteem, relationships and improving achievement.

Jessica Kingsley
116 Pentonville Road, London N1 9JB
020 78332307
020 78372917 (fax)
www.jkp.com

Jessica Kingsley publishes books for professional and general readers on a range of subjects. Their catalogue covers many topics such as autism, social work, working with offenders, asperger syndrome, disability, eating disorders and mental health.

Leeds Animation Workshop
45 Bayswater Row, Leeds LS8 5LF
0113 2484997 (tel/fax)
www.leedsanimation.demon.co.uk
email: law@leedsanimation.demon.co.uk

The Leeds Animation Workshop produces and distributes animated films on social issues such as communication difficulties between parents and their teenage children, racism and bullying in schools.

Mental Health Media
356 Holloway Road, London N7 6PA
020 77008171
020 76860959 (fax)
www.mhmedia.com
email: info@mhmedia.com

They produce a wide range of videos, DVD's, training packs and CD-ROMs for mental health service users.

Minority Rights Group International
54 Commercial Street, London E1 6LT
020 74224200
020 74224201 (fax)
www.minorityrights.org
minority.rights@mrgmail.org

The MRG catalogue includes books, postcards, photopacks, posters, training guides and autobiographical writings by refugees and minority students.

National Children's Bureau
8 Wakley Street, Islington, London EC1V 7QE
020 78436029
020 78436087 (fax)
www.ncb-books.org.uk
email: booksales@ncb.org.uk

NCB has a wide range of books, reports, training and development resources, CD-ROMs and videos to support professionals, parents, children and young people. Topics include services for young people, exclusion, ethnicity and children with special needs.

National Youth Agency
Eastgate House, 19-23 Humberstone Road, Leicester LE5 3GJ
0116 242 7427
0116 242 7444 (fax)
www.nya.org.uk
email: sales@nya.org.uk

The NYA is a major publisher of resources for those working with young people. Among the products are books on policy and practice, activity packs, posters, games, magazines and leaflets. Areas covered include disability issues, the extended school and youth and social policy.

Parentline Plus
520 Highgate Studios, 53-79 Highgate Road, Kentish Town, London, NW5 1TL
0800 783 6783
www.parentlineplus.org.uk
email: centraloffice@parentlineplus.org.uk

Parentline Plus is a UK registered charity which offers support for anyone parenting a child. The organisation publishes a range of materials on subjects such as family life, helping children learn, divorce and separation and truancy.

Pavilion Publishing Limited
The Ironworks, Cheapside, Brighton BN1 4GD
01273 623222
01273 625526 (fax)
www.pavpub.com
email: info@pavpub.com

They publish and distribute materials for both staff and service users in a variety of fields including learning disabilities, mental health and young people. They also run courses and conferences for professionals in health and social care.

The Rural Media Company
Sullivan House, 72-80 Widemarsh Street, Hereford HR4 9HG
01432 344039
01432 270539 (fax)
www.ruralmedia.co.uk
contact@ruralmedia.co.uk

The Rural Media Company works with marginalised groups on media projects and produces educational resources such as CD-ROMs, games, posters and videos. It particularly focuses on issues related to young people and its material covers emotional wellbeing, disability, 'race' and cultural diversity and sexual health and other issues.

Russell House Publishing Ltd
4 St Georges House, The Business Park, Uplyme Road,
Lyme Regis, Dorset DT7 3LS
01297 443948
01297 442948 (fax)
www.russellhouse.co.uk
email: help@russellhouse.co.uk

Their catalogue has books on subjects such as social policy and social care, working with young people and revitalising communities.

Sage Publications Ltd
1 Oliver's Yard, 55 City Road, London, EC1Y 1SP
020 73248500
020 73248600 (fax)
www.sagepub.co.uk
market@sagepub.co.uk

Sage publishes books, journals and electronic media on topics that include autism, communication, family studies and social work and social policy.

Sheffield Centre for HIV & Health
22 Collegiate Crescent, Sheffield S10 2BA
0114 2261904
www.sexualhealthsheffield.co.uk
email: chiv.admin@chs.nhs.uk

The centre has booklets for parents and teenagers, training packs, books and classroom activities on sexual health education for young people. The catalogue also includes videos on subjects such as the realities of sexual health services for young people and self-esteem.

Trust for the Study of Adolescence
23 New Road, Brighton, East Sussex BN1 1WZ
01273 693311
01273 679907 (fax)
www.tsa.uk.com
email: info@tsa.uk.com

TSA's primary commitment is to improving the lives of young people. Their catalogue has many TSA training materials, videos and books. It also includes board games, books and videos from outside suppliers. TSA publishes *Key Data on Adolescence* every two years.

Working With Men
320 Commercial Way, London SE15 1QN
020 83080709 (tel/fax)

Working with men produces publications, posters and games for workers wanting to develop their work with men. Their target areas are young men, health, domestic violence, sexual abuse, offending, fathering and men as carers.

Young Minds
102-108 Clerkenwell Road, London EC1M 5SA
020 73368445
020 73368446 (fax)
www.youngminds.org.uk

Young Minds produce booklets for young people on issues such as feeling depressed, dealing with anger, eating disorders and sexual abuse. They also have a range of leaflets for parents or professionals that offer information and support on mental health problems facing children and young people.

If the resource you are planning to use is 'live' such as a theatre group, there are useful good practice guidelines and tips on the following websites:

> http://www.hda-online.org.uk/documents/theatre_in_education.pdf
> http://www.rospa.org.uk/roadsafety/info/dramatic_impact.pdf